The Money-Spinners is the first t
how it is just possible, with skill a
– and win.

CW00434508

Jacques Black, an expert on prol
from most London casinos, uses his
past and present games of roulei
Through the true stories of those wr   .... gaming
tables, he explains how casino games can be beaten, what risks a gambler
should avoid, and the steps casinos may take when they spot a consistent
winner. For the mathematically inclined, a full appendix is included.

The Money-Spinners explains how the legendary William Nelson
Darnborough won a fortune at roulette in Monte Carlo; how Nick 'the
Greek' Dandalos won half a million dollars on the turn of a single card
at poker, but went on to lose several million dollars in his showdown
with Johnny Moss at Las Vegas in 1949; how in the early 1990s two
roulette scams at the Palm Beach and Golden Horsehoe casinos nearly
netted their perpetrators over a million pounds. And we see how the
principles of successful gambling can be applied far beyond the green
baize tables – in the worlds of finance, business and politics.

Since graduating from Oxford University with a First Class Honours
degree in Philosophy, Politics and Economics, the author has had a
varied international career. He has worked as an economist with the
government of St Lucia in the West Indies, as an investment banker in
Luxembourg, and as a senior executive in London Docklands. He cur-
rently works in Edinburgh as a management consultant.

Jacques Black has been barred from most London casinos for card
counting.

Extracts from reviews of the original edition of *The Moneyspinners*

"The pseudonymous author of this amusing and informative book on the mechanics, history and politics of gambling is at pains to disabuse us of one particular idea. That is: our cherished notion that today's professional card sharps resemble in any way the riverboat gamblers of old. These types are not flamboyant characters with ruffled shirts and pearl-handled revolvers stuck in their boot tops; rather they are men such as Lawrence Revere, who made a fortune playing blackjack and poker in Nevada and the casinos of the West Indies, who was deliberately and painstakingly inconspicuous, aiming to appear like an ordinary punter. The reason for this being the same as Jacques Black being a nom-de-plume. Namely, that if you reveal yourself to be a professional gambler in almost any casino in contemporary America or Britain, you will be barred."

– Will Self, *Sunday Times*, April 11 1993

"Whoever he may be, 'Black Jack' emerges as an engaging kind of guy. If I bump into him at the Victoria Casino, I hope he will make himself known – if not, alas, across the green baize."

– Anthony Holden (author of *Big Deal*), *Sunday Express*, April 18 1993

"This book is a compulsive read. There are numerous historical vignettes (usually of spectacular and rare successes) which are something of a joy to behold. An epilogue extends gambling theory into other fields – offering a novel reading of the career of Margaret Thatcher. And various appendices will ensure that you will at least be very knowledgeable when you hit the streets."

– Frank Kuppner, *Glasgow Herald*, April 21 1993

"Black's speciality is blackjack, a game that requires mathematical talent and card-money as well as strategy. The most interesting parts of his book are his arguments in favour of equal rights for card-counters, the protection of compulsive gamblers against themselves, and his proposal that 'casinos should become places of entertainment where any two or more individuals may sit down together to challenge each other to a non-physical game of chance or skill played for money.' There are also interesting appendices on the mathematics of blackjack."

– Al Alvarez (author of *The Biggest Game in Town*), *Daily Mail*, April 29 1993

"Professional gamblers are prepared to lose thousands without flinching. They are unquestionably a people obsessed. Any book on the subject written by a professional cannot fail to be touched by that obsession ... There is little doubt that 'Black' has not merely studied his methods with mathematical precision – as one might expect from his successes – he has also learnt from the ultimate practitioners of the art ... *The Moneyspinners* does provide a revelatory insight into this powerful demi-monde."

– Tom Rhodes, *Times*, May 20 1993

"The only casino game that players can legitimately win is blackjack or twenty-one. *The Moneyspinners* rehearses in detail the experience of the experts in this field. *The Moneyspinners* draws judiciously on a variety of well-known gambling sources. Gambling in casinos yields great pleasure, but it is only when the player can deliberately turn the odds in his favour – by judgement and experience – that gambling becomes profitable. As far as straight casino gambling goes, there is no such thing as easy money."

– David Spanier (author of *Easy Money: Inside the Gambler's Mind*),
Independent, May 20 1993

"Jacques Black has frequented the world's gaming watering holes and knows a thing or two about gaming in general, which he studies assiduously. So good is he at Blackjack that he has been barred from most London casinos for card counting. What is more, his scenario of scams and characters unfolds with the deadpan facts that comprise a fascinating read."

– Robin Lloyd, *Odds On*, July 1993

"Jacques Black was for a short spell the scourge of London casinos. Recognising quickly that roulette promised only poverty, Black became a blackjack king. He mastered the difficult art of card-counting, regarded by casino bosses as modern-day necromancy, and made a comfortable, if anti-social living. *The Moneyspinners* is a terrific read. It quickly delivers the bad news – that long term we haven't a hope in hell of winning at roulette – but softens the blow with the sweetener that it is possible to make blackjack pay. The only snag is you've got to be dedicated; you've got to be determined; and you've got to be damned clever. Card-counting is the key, but camouflage is also critical ... Black certainly knows his stuff and his book is essential reading for anyone trying to make casino betting pay."

– Derek McGovern (Sports Editor), *Racing Post*, March 7 1994

The Money-Spinners

*How Professional Gamblers Beat the Casinos
at Their Own Game*

JACQUES BLACK

OLDCASTLE BOOKS

First published in Great Britain by Faber & Faber, 1993

This edition published in 1998 by Oldcastle Books
18 Coleswood Road, Harpenden, Herts, AL5 1EQ

A CIP catalogue record for this book is available from the British Library.

ISBN 1-901982-07-6

2 4 6 8 10 9 7 5 3 1

Contents

'Even if gambling were altogether an evil, still on account of the very large number of people who play, it would seem to be a natural evil. Thus it is not absurd for me to discuss gambling, not in order to practise it, but in order to point out the advantages in it, and, of course, the disadvantages, so they may be reduced to a minimum.'

Gioralamo Cardono, *The Book of Dice Games*, c.1540

'It is a truth very certain that when it is not in our power to determine what is true, we ought to follow what is most probable.'

René Descartes, *Discourse on Method*

Acknowledgements

This book distils the ideas and adventures of many casino gamblers through the ages.

I owe a particular debt to three contemporary American authorities.

The first is Dr Edward Thorp, formerly of the University College of Los Angeles, whose 1962 book *Beat the Dealer* revolutionized the game of blackjack.

The second is Peter Griffin, professor at the California State University, Sacramento, who has researched the mathematics of casino games in greater depth than any other individual.

The third is Russell T. Barnhart of New York City, the world's leading authority on the history of casino gambling.

True Confessions of a Gambler

Once upon a time, I dreamt of becoming the finest blackjack player in Britain.

I became fascinated with the game after reading a basic text on card counting, *A Book on Casino Blackjack* by C. Ionescu Tulcea. I trained myself to count the cards as they were dealt according to the methods recommended by Tulcea. I then visited some of the low-stakes casinos around London's West End to put the principles into practice. They included the Golden Nugget in Shaftesbury Avenue, Charlie Chester's in Soho, and Napoleon's in Leicester Square. Later I was to be barred from them all, but at that time, early in my playing career, luck was with me and I won steadily.

This early success stimulated my interest in blackjack. I avidly studied the works of the authorities on the game, including the theoretical analyses of mathematicians such as Professors Edward Thorp and Peter Griffin, and the writings of professional gamblers who had earned their living from blackjack, including Lawrence Revere, Ken Uston and Stanford Wong.

Slowly a vision began to form. Perhaps I, too, could play blackjack as a business rather than as a mere pastime. I could renounce my life as a hired hand, and become a professional gambler beholden to no man. I would be able to play wherever and whenever I pleased.

I began to lay the basis for my future career. I read everything published on the game that was worth reading – and even more that was not worth reading. Through constant practice, I learnt how to count down a deck of cards in twelve seconds, and four decks within a minute. No matter how rapidly a dealer dealt the cards, I could count them faster. I learnt how to adjust the true count so that my betting and playing strategy would move up and down without conscious effort.

The true count measures the ratio of high cards (10s, court cards, and aces) to low cards waiting to be dealt. For reasons which will be explained, as this ratio rises, so the probability of a win for the player tends to increase. Conversely, when the ratio is low – that is, when there is a surplus of small cards such as 4s, 5s and 6s waiting to be dealt – the likelihood is that the dealer will win most hands. Accordingly, a skilful player will bet small amounts when the true count is low, and large amounts when the true count is high. He or she will also vary the playing strategy according to the proportion of high and low cards still to be dealt.

I spent many long hours of research on the mathematical problems that still appeared to be posed by the game. I identified an apparent discrepancy buried deep in the mathematical analyses of Professors Thorp and Griffin in the relationship posited between the true count and the player's advantage or disadvantage in the game – and resolved it, to my satisfaction at least, by concluding that the relationship between the true count and the player's advantage is non-linear.

For the interested reader, my ideas on the mathematics of casino games are explained in the appendices to this book.

I learnt of methods other than card counting which could assist the player in gaining an edge in blackjack. One such method involves observing the dealer as he or she shuffles the cards in order to establish the approximate location of clumps of high cards in the shuffled decks. If a blackjack player can track the shuffle accurately – an extremely difficult feat at the best of times – he or she can predict when the high cards favourable to the player are about to be dealt, and can place a large bet to take advantage of this knowledge.

My studies well advanced, I could enter most casinos in London in the confident knowledge that the laws of probability were on my side. There were only a few casinos where I felt I could not beat the game of blackjack because the conditions of play were so unfavourable.

I found that betting large amounts of money on the turn of a card did not unduly worry me. Even when things were running against me, I was certain it was only a negative deviation from an expected positive result, and that I would win out in the end.

This sublime state of affairs did not last. Playing blackjack day after day proved even more boring than working for a living. The expert blackjack player is the human being as computer, playing according to a well-defined repetitive algorithm. The algorithm runs as follows: first, count the cards as they are dealt. Then convert the running count into a true count by dividing by the number of cards remaining. Place your bet accordingly. If the true count is low, bet small; if it is high, bet large. When the cards have been dealt, use the true count to make appropriate adjustments to playing strategy. Watch the dealer play out his hand. Win-lose-tie. Place the bet for the next hand according to the advantage now indicated by the true count. Then repeat the process – count, adjust, play, bet; count, adjust, play, bet ... and so on and on, mechanically through deal after deal, shoe after shoe.

Once the techniques had been mastered, the intellectual challenge of the game was limited.

Occasionally taking a few days or weeks off meant that I could return to the casino refreshed and ready for battle. But it occurred to me that if I was dependent on the game for my livelihood, there was a limit to the number of unpaid breaks I could take – unless I was playing for such high stakes that a win of, say, 100 units would be sufficient to live on for a month.

Every now and then I began to chance my arm, and play on the £25 tables with the high rollers. But negative swings at these levels can run into several thousands or even tens of thousands of pounds. The risk of ruin is compounded by the even more serious risk of barring. Few gamblers play on the £25 tables, and those who do are closely scrutinized.

When I started playing blackjack, I regarded it as a series of mathematical puzzles to be solved, rather like the chess and bridge problems published in weekend newspapers. The money won or lost in the game was a means of testing the accuracy of my betting and playing decisions.

What I did not fully appreciate at that time was that the casinos do not see it quite like that. The casinos regard skilful blackjack players as cancers that must be cut out before they eat into casino profits. Casinos have no hesitation in barring any player they suspect is capable of gaining an edge in the game, whether through card counting or some other technique.

Little by little, the number of casinos in which I was permitted to exercise my skills began to diminish. There was a time when hardly a morning seemed to pass without a letter arriving from one club or another informing me that my membership had been terminated and that henceforth I would not be allowed in. Needless to say, these letters did not refund my membership fee, let alone the losses I had suffered at several of the casinos in question.

It seemed to be a no-win situation.

I conclude that I did not achieve my ambition of becoming Britain's best blackjack player. The best blackjack player in Britain would not merely have mastered the mathematics of the game, but would also have mastered the psychology of the casinos – dissimulating his or her skill so successfully that no casino would be aware there was a player at their tables capable of beating the game. This I failed to do.

For a brief period, I attempted to apply card-counting techniques to baccarat, otherwise known as punto banco. The gambler is not subjected to the same harassment playing this game as in blackjack because the casinos do not believe it can be beaten by mathematical methods. Neither, it must be said, do the mathematicians who are the world's leading authorities on casino games, Professors Edward Thorp and Peter Griffin. I am not so sure. What is certain is that the gambler's edge in the game is tiny and it occurs very infrequently. Waiting for a favourable situation to arise is tedious in the extreme.

I considered taking up poker seriously, but it wasn't the same. Winning modest sums from the casinos always provided some satisfaction, whereas winning from fellow gamblers simply wasn't as pleasurable. Losing was as unenjoyable as ever.

A further problem was the anti-social hours kept by gamblers. It is difficult to find a decent card game before sundown in London. Once you have found it, you must be prepared to play well into the small hours of the morning. Gamblers play when the rest of the world sleeps. They must therefore be single, separated, or have extremely tolerant spouses. Above all, casino gambling does not mix well with the responsibility of a young family.

Ironically, although the arrival of a family was to constrain my gambling activities, it also marked one of my greatest successes at the tables. During the early hours of the morning of Friday 18 August 1989 our first child was born. That evening, I left mother and baby in the hospital doing well. In my excitement, I felt disinclined to go back to an empty house, and drove instead to the Palm Beach Casino Club in Berkeley Street (this was in the days before I was barred from the Palm Beach).

I was at my peak as a blackjack player. My confidence had been boosted during the spring by solid wins on the 100 franc tables at Monte Carlo and Cannes. Emotionally and psychologically, I had never felt better.

Once I had settled down at the tables, my bet variations were smooth and intuitive as the true count fluctuated up and down. As for playing, my strategy varied with the card count with no more conscious thought than an experienced motorist gives to changing gear as he drives along.

That night, the cards were with me. They ran with the card count as smoothly as I have ever known. When the true count was high, out came the aces and 10s; when it was negative, the low cards followed faithfully. There was no dealer's bias – if anything, the cards seemed to run in the players' favour. Slowly but surely, first red and then black chips began to accumulate before me. Over the course of the next few hours, I enjoyed one of my most successful playing sessions at the card tables, winning more than I earned during many weeks of work in the City of London.

Emerging into Berkeley Square around 3 or 4 a.m. on Sunday morning, it seemed to me that the omens were clear. My newborn son would enjoy good fortune throughout his life, and would always bring good luck to those close to him. It was one of those moments of euphoria that all gamblers experience after a big win.

Later, when the excitement had passed, it would become clear that it was merely a mathematically predictable variation from the expected result, 'three or four standard deviations to the right', as Ken Uston would have put it. Yet at that moment, as I gazed up at the stars above Berkeley Square, it almost seemed as though, somewhere in the heavens, the spirits of Blaise Pascal, Abraham de Moivre and the Marquis de Laplace were smiling down at this triumph of the laws of mathematics over the cupidity of the casinos.

The Development of the Casino Industry

The State through the ages has always had difficulty in reconciling the anarchic, avaricious and frequently corrupt world of casino gambling with society's needs for stability and order.

The first person to resolve the dilemmas surrounding the State's attitude towards casino gambling was the Emperor Napoleon. In 1808 he signed a decree permitting gambling at the Palais Royal in Paris. The Palais thus became the first legal casino in Europe. In an astute compromise which helped to overcome moral objections, Napoleon stipulated that the proceeds of the taxes levied on gambling would be allocated to the construction of hospitals. Substantial funds were generated: between 1819 and 1837, the government earned 137 million francs from Parisian gaming clubs.

The Palais Royal was an enormous complex of shops, clubs, restaurants and cafés occupying six acres of prime land near the Louvre. It had been built by Cardinal Richelieu in 1642 and bequeathed to Louis XIII on his death. Louis XIII in turn passed it to Louis XIV, the Sun King, who found the Palais surplus to his requirements when he retired to Versailles and donated it to his nephew the Duke of Orleans as a wedding gift. It remained the home of the cadet branch of the Bourbon family until the French Revolution, when it was confiscated by the State and its rooms were leased out for business and pleasure.

The Palais Royal was an oasis of comfort:

There are 180 arches, and from each hangs a lantern. This is not a frivolous point. If you wanted to go and gamble someplace in the eighteenth century, you can imagine how dark Paris was. There were no gas lamps; there were very few police. Also it rained a great deal – still does – and it was so muddy that there were men who made a living carrying pedestrians across the streets. So one reason that the Palais Royal was so popular was that the rest of Paris was pretty grim to get around in ...

In the basement of the Palais Royal you could see actors, dwarves, giants, vetriloquists, dancing dogs, puppets, quack doctors, mountebanks, pornographers, an orchestra of blind musicians, and a restaurant. So you can see that it was a very exciting place ... There were huge slate sidewalks, where ten people could walk abreast; you can go round the shops and window-shop – you don't have to buy anything at the luxury shops; and if it rains, you can stay there – you have restaurants, you have the highest class courtesans who have rooms upstairs – it was the nicest place in town.

Barnhart, 'Gambling in Revolutionary Paris'

If the visitor was at a loss for something to do, there were four gaming clubs where he was offered roulette, dice and card games. If concerned about the moral implications of all this pleasure, he could always salve his conscience with the knowledge that a slice of the expenditure was contributing to the welfare of the sick.

Ironically, it was not the objections of the Church that led to the closure of the Palais Royal thirty years later, but the greed of surrounding businesses. The Palais was situated in what was then one of Paris's busiest commercial districts. Local businessmen observed that the spending power of visitors was being dissipated on the roulette wheels and card tables of the casinos, and concluded that if they were closed the money would flow through their shops instead. They began a campaign to close down the Palais Royal, and the restored Royalist government responded to their demands.

At midnight on 31 December 1837, four casinos in the Palais Royal and three other casinos in Paris were closed among scenes of riotous disorder.

Unfortunately for the local burghers, the closure of the casinos did not boost their businesses. It was an early case of killing the goose that laid the golden egg. After gambling ceased at the Palais Royal, visitors no longer flocked to the area. Trade and commerce slumped, and the businesses of many who had campaigned for the closure of the Palais went bankrupt.

Within a few years the Palais Royal became a moribund place. As the throngs of gamblers no longer came to patronize its cafés and elegant restaurants, one by one they were all closed down, leaving today only the Restaurant Grand Velour. The shops in the galleries, once so crowded, were soon bereft of a single customer, so that most of the shopkeepers gave up and moved out to the livelier avenues of the city. The Palais Royal had become as quiet and forlorn as a cathedral close and has remained so to this day. A few footfalls in the arcades, the flutter of pigeons, the cries of a handful of toddlers watched by dozing governesses of a sunny afternoon – such are the ghostly remnants of the enthusiastic throngs of yesteryear.

'Gambling in Revolutionary Paris'

Others were not slow to seize upon the myopia of the merchants of Paris. New casinos opened in several independent mid-European duchies, including Baden-Baden, Luxembourg and Homburg. Many of the proprietors of the Parisian casinos simply moved their enterprises elsewhere. They included Antoine Chabert, the owner of one of the casinos in the Palais Royal, who opened four clubs in the Duchy of Nassau; Jacques Benazet, former proprietor of the Frascati club, who in 1838 took over the lease of the Conversation House in Baden-Baden; and the twin brothers Blanc, François and Louis. When the Parisian casinos were closed down, the Blanc brothers opened a small casino in the Grand Duchy of Luxembourg in 1838, before moving on to Hesse-Homburg in 1842. They there established the Kursaal, which for the next thirty years was to be perhaps the most famous of all continental gaming houses.

In 1842 Homburg was unknown. In the vicinity of the landgrave's castle had accumulated a few hundred houses over the centuries. It was a peaceful and forgotten town. There was a single inn called the Eagle where a few German families stayed in the summer to drink the mineral waters and live cheaply.

Having failed recently in a venture in France, the two Blanc brothers arrived in Homburg. Their commercial stock consisted of only a roulette wheel, a few thousand franc notes, and an ex-croupier from Frascati in Paris. François Blanc got an immediate audience with the landgrave's prime minister, and was given permission to set up the roulette wheel in one of the private chambers of the Eagle.

So successful was the summer's business that in the fall François Blanc obtained the exclusive concession to build a Kursaal (casino), lay out a public garden, and pay the landgrave's treasury $16,000 a year. The town streets were paved and illuminated with gas lights. Now in 1868 the surrounding hills have numerous villas. There are more than four hundred and fifty acres of gardens, 10,000 annual visitors, twenty hotels and a hundred furnished houses.

London *Daily News*, 1868

When Prussia defeated Austria in the Austro-Prussian War of 1866, it annexed several formerly independent states, including Hesse-Homburg. After a six-year stay of execution, the Prussian government and its allies closed all the casinos under their jurisdiction at 11 p.m. on 31 December 1872.

Count Corti recounted the last days of the Kursaal in his memoirs:

In spite of a very hard winter, crowds of foreigners arrived to see the end of play. The gaming salons were crowded every night, and everybody staked high in the hope that luck might favour him at the last moment.

Finally the last evening arrived. Gamblers stood six to seven deep around the tables. At exactly five minutes to eleven the croupier announced in a voice that trembled slightly: 'Gentlemen, place your bets ... the last ... for ever!' The table was piled high with innumerable bets. The roulette wheel turned, and the supervisor announced: 'Twenty, black, even, and high!' and play was at an end in Homburg.

Der Zauberer von Homburg und Monte Carlo

The consequences of the Kursaal's closure were catastrophic for the town. Just as with the closure of the Palais Royal, the flow of visitors dried to a trickle. In 1873 the novelist Henry James took a room in an inn in the mountains near Homburg and noted that the town appeared almost completely deserted.

The feelings of the surviving Blanc twin, François, forced to close his casino operation for the second time in his life, may be imagined. But gamblers are nothing if not adaptable, and François already had his eye on another site. It was in an obscure, impoverished principality of eight square miles on the south-eastern shore of France. Hemmed in by the Maritime Alps and facing the Mediterranean Sea, the principality was virtually cut off from the rest of the world. Little had changed since a German traveller, one Dr Sulzer, had attempted to reach it overland from Nice a century earlier.

The path is painful beyond words and would dishearten even goats. In some way or other one must clamber along the face of cliffs, as abrupt as the roofs of our German churches, and fight tooth and nail to keep one's foothold ... The path, called 'the Cornish Road', is so narrow that a single mule occupies its whole width; in addition, while a rider's left knee scrapes against the rocks, his right dangles over a precipice which gives him vertigo.

Barnhart, *Gamblers of Yesteryear*

In such unpromising terrain did François Blanc establish what was to become the most famous casino in the world.

When he arrived in the principality of Monaco, François Blanc was determined that the story of the Palais Royal and the Homburg Kursaal would not be repeated. This time he wanted to establish a casino that could not be closed on a politician's whim. Accordingly, on the principle that if you can't beat them you must join them, he made the principality of Monaco itself a shareholder in his new enterprise.

So it was that the Société des Bains de Mer was formed. It still exists today, a century and a quarter later, and its revenues have transformed Monaco from one of the poorest into one of the wealthiest regions of Europe. In addition to establishing the Grand Casino de Monte Carlo, the Société promoted hotels and restaurants, built gardens and promenades, and sponsored a wide range of entertainments to amuse visitors to the principality.

When François Blanc died in 1877, he bequeathed to his son Camille the directorship of an already prospering enterprise. By the end of the nineteenth century, the Grand Casino regularly entertained up to 10,000 visitors a day, and its place as the unchallenged centre of casino gambling in Europe was secure.

Denied many alternative venues, Europe's aristocracy converged upon Monte Carlo each spring and summer. The casino's records reveal that William Ewart Gladstone regularly spent his vacation there, as did the heir to the throne, Edward Prince of Wales. When he later became King Edward VII, his son George kept up the tradition by also visiting the Grand Casino. The casino's records reveal that another visitor during the Edwardian era was the young Winston Churchill, who won $780 there in 1910 shortly before he was appointed Home Secretary. Churchill visited Monte Carlo on several other occasions over the next half century. His last recorded visit was in 1960, when he won $335 at the tables.

While Prime Ministers, potentates and princes played at Monte Carlo, the humble proletariat were effectively excluded by the costs of travel and the high stakes. In the inter-war years the development of casinos on the coasts of Normandy and Flanders, in towns such as Deauville, Dieppe and Ostend, made casino games more accessible to the prosperous middle classes in southern England. Working-class gamblers were not catered for by casinos until the development of Las Vegas.

Nevada legalized casino gambling in 1931, and was the only state of the union where casinos were allowed until they were legalized in New Jersey half a century later. During the 1930s, the Nevada casino industry was concentrated in Reno, and Las Vegas was little more than a village in the desert where travellers rested on their way to somewhere else. But during the war years of the early 1940s, the town caught the attention of a certain Benjamin Siegel, whose dream was, as he put it, 'to build the biggest goddamned casino in the world!'

Siegel had successfully set up a racing wire between the east and west coasts of the United States on behalf of the Bud Meier mob, otherwise known as Murder Incorporated. With funds drawn from the profits of the racing wire and his various associates, Siegel was able to transform his dream into reality, and in 1945 his extravagant Flamingo Club became the first major casino in Las Vegas.

In its early years, the Flamingo marked up another first – the first recorded case of a large casino that succeeded in consistently losing money. Siegel was swindled by his clientele and staff alike. His career came to an abrupt end in 1947 when he was gunned down by a person or persons unknown. It has been suggested that the perpetrators of this crime may not have been entirely unconnected with certain disgruntled investors in the Flamingo. Be that as it may, it is undeniable that after the change of management enforced by Siegel's demise, the fortunes of the Flamingo began to improve.

The development of the Flamingo had a catalytic impact on the development of Las Vegas. Little by little, as its initial problems were overcome, it drew other developments along in its wake. Siegel's dream of transforming Las Vegas into the world's greatest casino resort survived him. By the early 1960s Las Vegas had overtaken Monte Carlo in terms of revenues and visitor numbers. As the American novelist Tom Wolfe drily observed in 'Las Vegas', an essay written in the early 1960s,

Las Vegas has become just as Bugsy Siegel dreamed: the American Monte Carlo, without the inevitable upper-class baggage of the Riviera casinos. In Monte Carlo, there is still the plush mustiness of nineteenth-century noble lines. At Monte Carlo there are still wrong forks, deficient accents, poor tailoring, gauche displays, nouveaux richness, cultural aridity – concepts unknown in Las Vegas.

Britain, meanwhile, was being left behind in the worldwide growth of the casino industry. Towards the end of the 1950s, as Harold Macmillan informed Britons that they had never had it so good, it was beginning to occur to the British Government that some of this new-found affluence was being siphoned out of the official economy into illicit gambling activities. Much to the regret of government officials, the fact that politicians and moralists decreed that gambling was a bad thing had not prevented Britons from indulging in the occasional flutter. Not only were those who could afford it able to travel to Monaco, France or Belgium to indulge their vice, but private games and illegal bookmaking enterprises were increasingly common in Britain itself.

In an attempt to get a slice of the action, the government reluctantly legalized gambling in the early 1960s. An explosion of casino developments ensued. At its peak, in the mid-1960s, it was estimated that there were more than one and a half thousands casinos open in Britain. When it came to the government's notice that the Inland Revenue was not always getting its fair share of gaming revenues, the Gaming Board's powers were strengthened and licensing requirements tightened up. A further shake-up occurred in the early 1980s following a fierce competitive war between London casinos.

Despite these problems, during the first twenty-five years following legalization London established itself as the most important European centre of casino gambling. In terms of gross casino revenues, London ranks third in the world after Nevada and Atlantic City in the United States. More money is wagered in London casinos than in other European centres such as Deauville or Monte Carlo.

Much of the credit for the growth in the UK casino industry must go to the Gaming Board, which has eliminated any criminal element from casino gambling and kept the games clean and free of cheating. Many of its licensing provisions are positively beneficial for the gambler – for example, the provision that no alcohol be served in the gaming area. This restriction must have saved many an imprudent gambler from himself. However, in recent years the London casino industry has suffered a relative decline as new casinos have been developed in tourist resorts in continental Europe, including Greece and Portugal. It is possible that some of the restrictions imposed by the Gaming Board have contributed to London's decline.

For example, blackjack is the most rapidly growing casino game worldwide; yet Britain now offers one of the most adverse environments in the world for playing the game. The rules of blackjack as offered in British casinos are highly unfavourable to the player by international standards. The player employing perfect basic strategy against a randomly shuffled shoe of cards and placing flat bets faces a disadvantage of

−0.65 per cent against the British game. By comparison, in casinos in Belgium, France and Monaco where I have played, the rules are more generous and the basic strategy player is at a disadvantage of only between −0.25 and −0.50 per cent. This may appear insignificant, but over a long series of plays it can make the difference of many thousands of pounds.

The Gaming Board supports the casino policy of barring the tiny minority of blackjack players who are able to overcome the adverse rules and gain a small edge in the game of blackjack. A player has no right of appeal. The Gaming Board's line in these matters appears to be that casinos can only offer games of pure chance rather than skill. However, if it were to be consistent in this policy, it would have to prohibit blackjack altogether, since at any level of play the outcome of the game is influenced by the skill with which the player exercises the choices available. Indeed, that is the main attraction of blackjack compared to other casino games.

Business magazine of August 1989 put forward the following view of the recession in the London casino industry.

Max Kingsley of London Clubs, an experienced casino manager who runs the Ritz Casino, believes that there are too many casinos in London. While still the world's casino capital, it no longer dominates the international gambling business in the way that it once did. New casinos are opening, especially around the Mediterranean, and turnover is falling. The British Casino Association reports that in the year ending 31 March 1989, the amount gambled in London casinos fell by 7.2 per cent to £1.1 billion.

The solution proposed by Mr Kingsley is to restrict competition and limit the number of new casinos opening in London. For this reason, his London Clubs group objected to a casino licence application by John Aspinall in 1991.

My own view is that what is needed in the British gaming industry is not less competition, but more. This in turn requires less regulation by the Gaming Board. Lack of competition, combined with the tight regulatory framework, are threatening London's position as the leading centre of casino gambling in Europe because genuine high-rolling international gamblers are deserting London for more attractive venues where the rules and conditions are often more liberal.

The Gaming Board should continue to control the licensing of casino operators tightly to ensure that cowboys and crooks are kept out of the industry and only reputable companies are awarded licenses. It should also adopt the policy of the gaming authorities of the province of Alberta, and provide that no gambler be excluded from membership of a casino simply because he or she is seeking to gain an edge in casino games by skilful methods such as card counting or shuffle tracking.

Any gambler barred from a casino should have a right to appeal to the Gaming Board. In cases of genuine cheating, the physical evidence provided by biased equipment and modern video surveillance would provide sufficient evidence to support a prohibition. Genuine cheats who seek to fix the games by physically interfering with gaming equipment or gambling chips should be barred. Where a gambler has been barred merely because he was winning, however, the Gaming Board could insist that the player's membership be reinstated as a condition of the casino's licence.

In other respects, the degree of regulation should be reduced. Once an operator has gained a licence, that operator should be permitted to decide on the games he provides and the rules he offers for those games. Deregulation would enable more enlightened casino owners to offer better rules and playing conditions. The gambling press could advise gamblers as to which casinos offer the best odds in their games, as the *Racing Post* does for sporting events. Casinos could also sponsor other games – not only poker, but also backgammon, chess, bridge and other card games. Casinos should become places of entertainment where any two or more individuals may sit down together to challenge each other to a non-physical game of chance or skill played for money. By providing such facilities, casinos would not be placed in the adversarial position against the gambler they presently occupy. Rather, they would hire out gaming facilities for a pre-determined fee, or would organize competitions where their return was a slice of the pot.

As people's leisure time and disposable income continue to rise, the potential demand for such facilities will increase. A liberal policy, freed of the present constraints imposed by Gaming Board regulations, would help to stimulate competition and innovation and restore London's pre-eminence in the gambling world. The only two restrictions that should be imposed by the Gaming Board are that any company applying for a gaming licence should be rigorously vetted so that the credentials of its directors would be proved; and that any gambler, other than a proven cheat, should be permitted to play in any licensed casino.

These reforms would mean that international high rollers would be attracted back, and more social gamblers would be encouraged to enjoy casino games. The fact casinos would no longer have the right to bar the small number of gamblers capable of beating the game of blackjack by skill would be offset many times over by the greater revenues generated by an open and friendly environment.

There is one more aspect of the casinos' policy on which I would like to touch: their attitude towards compulsive gambling. The casinos take the line that they are places of entertainment, and for that reason they bar professional gamblers, yet they do not bar compulsive gamblers. Anyone acquainted with compulsive gamblers knows that they do not play for fun, but are driven to gamble by an addiction that can be as destructive as any alcohol or drugs. During the course of my playing career I have come across compulsive gamblers who have lost everything through their addiction, including their homes and their families, as they descended into bankruptcy. The casinos in which they played were well aware that they were betting far, far more than they could afford to lose. Yet, in contrast to the ruthless counter-measures taken against any gambler suspected of being able to gain even the smallest edge for the lowest stakes, the casinos let these tragic individuals continue to play until they had lost everything they had.

The British casino industry is riddled with such double standards. There are enough people for whom a few hundred or a few thousand pounds lost on the gaming tables can be written off as small change for the casinos to make an adequate return without driving to ruin those who cannot afford to lose, but who are compelled by psychological problems to go on gambling.

ROULETTE

Into the Lion's Den

Casinos may be defined as business enterprises that seek to relieve their clients of their cash as rapidly and painlessly as possible. In return, they offer the gambler only the dubious entertainment of winning or (more likely) losing money in games of chance where the odds are stacked against him. So, the best advice that can be offered to anyone considering going into a casino is: don't.

Failing this, the second best piece of advice is: if you must go into a casino, only take with you money that you can afford to lose. Leave your chequebooks, credit cards, and cashpoint plastic at home. Take only a return bus or train ticket, so that if the worst happens and you are cleaned out, you can at least make your way home to lick your wounds in peace. Don't leave yourself any alternative. Don't give yourself access to cash or credit to go on gambling after your bankroll has been lost. Your luck will not change; you will only lose more money than you ever intended.

The best way to resist that temptation is to avoid it.

If you are still determined to enter a casino, the third piece of advice is to know precisely the odds of any casino game in which you participate, and to respect those odds. The guiding principle of this book, and of all successful gambling, is: *respect the odds, and they will respect you.*

The odds in all the games offered by the casino are against the player and in favour of the house. The house percentage is not great – on a number in single-zero roulette, for example, the house enjoys an advantage of approximately 2.7 per cent. This is because the bank pays 35–1 if the number comes up (£35 for every £1 bet placed by the player) and returns the gambler's original stake, so that gambler gets a gross return of £36 on a winning £1 bet. However, there are 37 numbers on a roulette wheel (numbers 1 to 36 inclusive, plus the zero), so on average over a long series of trials the gambler would expect to wager £1 on 37 occasions for each time his number came up. Thus, the gambler would have to bet £37 to win £36 – a negative return of $\frac{1}{37}$ or approximately 2.7 per cent.

Although the house's percentage is not great, over a long enough period it is certain to be decisive. A player may have a lucky streak where the bets win more often than would be expected by reference to their true probability. But the longer play goes on, the more likely it is that the actual results will reflect the mathematical probabilities. This is because of what statisticians term the law of large numbers, which states that the larger the number of tests of any series of independent trials, the more likely it is that the actual results of those tests will approximate the expected mathematical result.

To illustrate this principle, consider the case of the alternate red and black numbers on a roulette wheel, which are broken only by the zero. It is perfectly possible that, in a hundred spins of the roulette wheel, a red number could come up ninety times. I would be prepared to bet that such a result has been recorded under actual casino conditions. It is unlikely, but it would be within the parameters of a normal statistical deviation around the average outcome (which would approximate to 49 reds, 49 blacks, and 2 zeros in 100 spins of the wheel).

However, as the number of trials rises, the probability of the ball landing on a red number 90 per cent of the time diminishes. I am prepared to bet that, in 100,000 spins, there has never been a result of 90,000 red numbers on any roulette wheel in any casino in the world. Such a result would not be normal statistical deviation; it would cause us to question the fairness of the roulette wheel in question.

Over 100,000 spins of the wheel, it is possible to predict with some accuracy what the outcome will be. A red number will come up about 48,650 times, as will a black number. A zero will come up 2,700 times (or on 1 spin in 37). There will be some deviation from these figures, but in percentage terms the deviation will not be significant.

There are few attested stories of consistently successful casino gamblers. Those there are indicate that the few people who have consistently won money at casino games have known precisely the true odds of the games at which they have played, and have respected those odds. Another common feature of successful gamblers is that they played systematically, and their systems incorporated information about the odds of the games they beat. In other words, they played scientifically, not randomly. They owed their success to mathematics rather than the fickle charms of Lady Luck.

Successful gamblers in fact do not really gamble at all, in the dictionary sense of playing games of chance. They take calculated risks over a long series of trials knowing that, on balance, the probabilities favour them rather than the house.

Take the famous story of the man who broke the bank at Monte Carlo. William Jaggers was a British engineer who travelled down to Monaco in the late nineteenth century armed with a simple but powerful idea. His idea was this. In roulette, the percentages favour the house, but only very slightly. The player may win over a short period but cannot win in the long term, provided that the odds against any number coming up are 36–1 while the payout ratio is only 35–1. If that is the case, the law of large numbers will conspire to grind even the luckiest gambler into a loser in the long run.

But what would happen if the true chance of particular numbers coming up was less than 36–1? If there were some way of predicting, even very approximately, where the roulette ball was going to land, then the odds would shift decisively away from the house and in favour of the player. If the player could be certain that just two numbers on the roulette wheel would not come up, he or she could cover the remaining 35 numbers with £1 bets, and win £35 on the number that actually came up, plus the original £1 bet, to realize a net profit of £1 on each spin of the wheel. The normal odds would be turned on their head. Instead of the casino having an advantage of 2.7 per cent, the player has an advantage of nearly 2.9 per cent, winning £1 for every £35 bet. Over a long enough period, such an advantage could turn a pauper into a millionaire.

Jaggers hired six clerks to record a month of winning numbers on the roulette wheels of the Grand Casino at Monte Carlo. In the quiet of his hotel room, Jaggers studied the results, calculated variances in the frequency with which the roulette ball landed on different groups of numbers, and came to the conclusion that some of the roulette wheels were biased. As a professional engineer himself, Jaggers was aware that few feats of engineering are perfect and that the roulette wheel was no exception. Even a slight tilt imperceptible to the human eye would, over a long period, tend to influence the ball into certain segments of the wheel.

Armed with this knowledge, Jaggers simply backed the areas of the wheel in which the ball was more likely to land. With his research complete, the execution of the plan was mechanical. His spread of bets might win or lose, but he knew that on average he would win more often than he would lose, and with careful money management he could not fail to accumulate large amounts of cash.

He went on to win 1.5 million francs before the casino management realized his gains were due to something more than a run of luck and replaced the biased wheels.

Jaggers had applied the first rule of any successful gambler. He had quietly and methodically assessed the true odds of the game, and bet only when those odds exceeded the odds actually being offered. He bet when the odds were in his favour rather than against him. It is also safe to assume that he followed a prudent money management system so that he would not be wiped out by freak runs, such as the occurrence of 90 red numbers in 100 spins of the roulette wheel.

In 1947, two students at the California Institute of Technology, Albert Hibbs and Roy Walford, emulated Jaggers' methods at the Palace and Harold's Club in Reno, Nevada. Applying statistical techniques to distinguish biased from unbiased wheels, they established that approximately one wheel in four exhibited a bias sufficient to overcome the house edge. In the course of a single session they applied this information to clear a profit of $7,000. In the following year they applied the same methods with equal success at the Golden Nugget in Las Vegas.

Could their coup be repeated today? It is possible, although with technological advances the chances of finding a biased roulette wheel are slim. Casinos take great care to make sure their games are set up in such a way that not even the smartest gambler could gain a consistent edge over them. In addition, casinos periodically change their roulette wheels, so that there is no certainty that a biased wheel will remain in operation long enough for a statistician to take advantage of it.

Even if some slight bias did exist, it would take many hours of painstaking research to identify and quantify it. This is precisely what Jaggers and the Hibbs-Walford team did before they placed a single bet. It gives the lie to the popular image of the successful gambler as a flamboyant extrovert who plays with money in a careless, devil-may-care fashion. The successful gambler is more likely to be a self-controlled introvert who takes care to be noticed as little as possible and whose success is based on a cool, rational assessment of the true odds of any game in which he or she participates.

Some years after Jaggers' triumph another, even more interesting, visitor arrived at Monte Carlo with a system to beat the roulette wheel.

The Greatest Roulette Player
Ever to Hit Monte Carlo?

The True Story of William Nelson Darnborough

William Nelson Darnborough was an American adventurer who lived on his wits after graduating from Normal University, Illinois, around the year 1890. For a time he made his living by playing professional baseball, and when he retired from the game he found that he could not settle into the routine of a nine-to-five job. Instead he set up a roulette wheel in a Chicago bar. However, one day a well-heeled gambler arrived at the bar and cleaned out Darnborough during the course of the evening with a succession of winning coups.

Penniless, Darnborough joined a travelling circus; but his interest in the game that had ruined him remained. He acquired another roulette wheel and spent many hours studying its mechanical laws of motion. He travelled through California with his roulette wheel, gradually restoring his fortunes in a series of games against all-comers. From California he travelled to Latin America, and thence, in 1904, to Monte Carlo. He was thirty-five years old. His exploits were recorded by the Hon. S. R. Beresford:

An American named Darnborough enriched himself to the extent of 83,000 pounds from the Monte Carlo casino alone ... He undoubtedly broke all records for continuous gain, for every shilling of his money was won on the numbers at roulette.

Mr Darnborough was probably the most remarkable man, so far as gambling is concerned, that ever passed into the casino at Monte Carlo. Never before or since have such masses of gold and notes been heaped upon a roulette table. The most astonishing feature of his operations was the lightning speed with which he placed his stakes. He would commence to stake his money when the croupier commenced to spin, continuing to dab the board with piles of money ... It was truly wonderful to watch him ambidextrously at work; one hand would have been altogether insufficient for his purpose, so both hands were engaged at lightning speed in shovelling from the reserves to the section of operation.

A Reuters dispatch on 14 December 1910, published in the London *Evening Telegraph*, stated that

Mr Darnborough leaves Monte Carlo for London today with winnings of £64,000 from one month's stay. He began with a capital of £1,200. He won up to £93,000 at his peak. He won from £12,000 to £16,000 a day. He left feeling his luck was at an end.

But was it just luck? Darnborough never gave any further explanation of his winnings, yet it seems inconceivable that his run of success was due to an amazing run of luck against the odds.

Having made a fortune at the tables of Monte Carlo, in 1911 Darnborough wooed and wed a beautiful English heiress named Frances Erskine. She consented to marry him only on the condition that he would never gamble again. Darnborough accepted this condition, and the two of them settled down to a comfortable existence as members of the landed gentry in southern England. He died in 1958 at the age of ninety and took the secret of how he beat the roulette wheel with him to the grave.

There are, however, a few clues which enable us to form a hypothesis. In an article written by a Mr C. N. Williamson in *McClure's Magazine* in February 1913, entitled 'Systems and System Players at Monte Carlo', we find this description of Darnborough:

The greatest sensation of modern days has been made for several seasons running by an American – young, clean-shaven, keen-eyed, pale-faced . . . When he won vast sums, he did not smile; when he lost, his expression never changed.

His play was on numbers but seemed to vary from time to time, occasionally being for 'repeats', often skipping from one side of the wheel to the other. No one could understand what he was doing, though it was evident he had a system of some sort, as he staked without hesitation. The American often lost, but his wins were immensely higher than his losses.

The whole table had to wait while he plastered it with numerous piles of gold, and wait again while he was being paid. But the interested crowd was never impatient, and the 'system' remained a mystery until at last, when the lucky player left Monte Carlo with $400,000 of the bank's money, mysterious gossip began to fly about.

The gossip to which Mr Williamson refers was that Darnborough had 'inside information' which enabled him to predict where the roulette ball was going to land. This information was apparently relayed to him by an assistant who was always with him at the tables and 'signalled to the player at the last instant into which quarter of the cylinder the ball seemed likely to fall'.

I do not believe that this explanation of Darnborough's success is tenable. Anyone who has played roulette will appreciate the difficulty of predicting where the ivory roulette ball will land when it is in motion. The notion that Darnborough had an assistant who could do just that, and who could then signal to Darnborough in which segment of the wheel the ball would land, and that Darnborough would then have time to place his bets accordingly – all this, without being detected by the casino personnel – stretches credulity beyond its limits.

Nevertheless, it does seem likely that Darnborough could predict where the ball was going to land with sufficient accuracy to swing the odds decisively away from the house and in his own favour. I believe that he made his prediction on the basis of his own observations *at the moment the roulette ball left the croupier's hand.* Note a key phrase in Beresford's account of Darnborough's method: 'He would commence to stake his money when the croupier commenced to spin.'

More than seventy years after Darnborough left Monte Carlo for the last time, the great theoretician of gambling Edward O. Thorp explained how such a system might work. Thorp describes how he hit upon the system in his chapter on roulette in *The Mathematics of Gambling.* As an impoverished physics graduate at the University College of Los Angeles, California, he 'began to toy with the fantasy that I could shatter the chains of poverty through a scientifically-based winning gambling system'.

Thorp relates how his fantasy began to be transformed into reality during the course of an afternoon's discussion with some fellow students at UCLA.

The conversation turned to fantasies of easy money. We began to speculate on whether there was a way to beat the roulette wheel. We kicked around the idea of whether croupiers could control where the ball will land well enough to significantly affect the odds, and concluded that this is impossible under the usual conditions of the game. It was a short brainstorming step to wonder whether wheels were imperfect enough to change the odds to favour the player. Those in the group who 'knew' assured me that the wheels are veritable jewelled watches of perfection, carefully machined, balanced and maintained. This is false. Wheels are sometimes imperfect enough so that they can be beaten. I had no experience with gambling, so I accepted the mechanical perfection of roulette wheels.

But mechanical perfection, for a physicist, means predictability . . . Suddenly the orbiting roulette ball seemed like the planets in their stately and precise paths . . . In the following weeks the idea kept coming back to me: measure the position and velocity of the roulette ball at a fixed time and you can then predict its future path, including when and where the ball will spiral into the rotor. Measure the rotor's position and velocity at a fixed time, and you can predict the rotor's rotation for any future time. But then you will know what section of the rotor will be there when the ball arrives. So you know (approximately) what number will come up!

You can see that the system requires that bets be placed *after* the ball and rotor are set in motion and somehow timed.

Over the next few years, Thorp did more research on the theoretical path of a roulette ball around the central rotor, and developed a computer model that could predict the path and likely landing area of the ball. His research was interrupted by his work on blackjack, but he returned to it in the 1960s. At that point, he discovered complications that would make precise prediction of where a roulette ball would land impossible. The most important complication arose because of the frets which divide the numbered pockets.

Sometimes the ball will hit a fret and bounce several pockets on, other times it will be knocked backwards. Or it may be stopped dead. Occasionally the ball will bounce out to the edge of the rotor and move most of a revolution there before falling back into the inner rings of pockets. Thus, even if we knew where the ball would enter the rotor, the 'spattering' from the frets causes considerable uncertainty regarding where it finally stops. This tells you that successful physical prediction can at most forecast in which *sector* of the wheel the ball will end.

We are back to the world of probabilities, not certainties. However, Thorp persevered with his research, and found some compensating advantages. The velocity of the rotor driving the roulette wheel changes very slowly, so it is possible to predict quite accurately which segment of the wheel will correspond to the point at which the roulette ball leaves the circumference of the wheel. Experimentation indicated that the random disturbance imparted by the frets between the numbers was not sufficient to totally destroy predictability. It was therefore still possible to forecast the segment into which the ball would fall with sufficient accuracy to overcome the casino's edge.

However, Thorp was doubtful whether any prediction of where the roulette ball would land would be sufficiently accurate to overcome the house edge under casino conditions. The reason for his scepticism was the variability in the three factors necessary for prediction: the rotor velocity; the speed of the roulette ball; and the initial position of the rotor when the croupier launches the ball. The last two factors depend critically on the croupier, who is unlikely, in Thorp's view, to spin the ball with constant force or from a constant location in relation to its last landing place.

In addition, Thorp found that the deflecting vanes on the side of the rotor add considerable randomness to the outcome, as do the frets or spacers between the pockets.

His gloomy conclusion was,

I don't believe that any dealer is predictable enough to cause a root square mean error of less than 17 pockets (which is the critical mean error that must not be exceeded if the player is to be able to overcome the house advantage). [However] if a dealer dutifully practised spinning a ball a fixed number of revolutions, and if a motor spun the rotor at a constant velocity, and we have a very good way of deciding exactly which number is opposite the ball just as it is released, it might be barely possible to give a small prediction advantage. I consider even that very unlikely.

On the basis of his detailed research, Thorp's scientific scepticism about the feasibility of predicting where the roulette ball will land appears well founded. Nevertheless, it is my contention that this is precisely what William Nelson Darnborough achieved, without the aid of Thorp's computer. Note that the key elements in his system were to place his bets *after* the ball had been launched, and to place them in such a way as to cover a *physical segment* of the roulette wheel. In other words, he was predicting the physical area of the wheel in which the ball was likely to land.

Supporting evidence for the hypothesis chat the roulette wheel is, at least theoretically, beatable by the laws of physics has been provided by Thomas Bass in his book *The Newtonian Casino*. This book tells the story of Eudaemonic Enterprises, a disparate group of gamblers, physicists and computer scientists who sought to develop a computer capable of predicting the path and landing place of a roulette ball.

Ironically, their endeavour was inspired by a casual remark by Dr Thorp towards the end of his 1960 book *Beat the Dealer*, indicating that there were several people including himself who possessed a method of beating roulette wheels whether or not they were defective.

As we have seen, twenty years later Dr Thorp confessed that his early hopes for the development of a winning roulette system had been dashed. But the associates of Eudaemonic Enterprises were not aware of Dr Thorp's failure. They concluded on the basis of their early research that a computer could be developed capable of predicting where a roulette ball would land. They put in several years of work to design an algorithm for the orbit of a roulette ball and its descent to the wheel. They then translated this algorithm into a computer program and designed a computer small enough to be concealed in the heel of a shoe. Finally, they trained individuals to use the computer under actual casino conditions.

Their attempt to physically predict the path and landing place of a roulette ball was impeded by the random elements of the game imparted by the scatter and bounce of the ball.

Scatter results from the fact that the roulette balls, after dropping from orbit, sometimes find their trajectory interrupted by metal diamonds attached to the sloping side, or stator, of the roulette wheel. *Bounce* refers to the problem of balls hopping from cup to cup on the central disk, or rotor, before finally coming to rest. Bounce and scatter tend to randomize the game.

The associates of Eudaemonic Enterprises discovered further factors affecting the game. Three in particular were important: the density of the roulette ball; the degree of friction and wind resistance it encountered on its path around the wheel; and the tilt of the wheel. However, unlike Dr Thorp, Eudaemonic Enterprises were able to successfully incorporate the effects of tilt, bounce, scatter and drag into a series of equations.

These equations were translated into a computer program. The program incorporated parameters for the velocity of the central rotor, ball deceleration, and time of fall. It was initiated by clicking in the speed of the ball at fixed points on its journey around the roulette wheel. This final piece of information was entered by a data collector, who clicked with his or her toe when the roulette ball passed a fixed point of the wheel, say the zero. Sequential clicks would enable the microprocessor to compute the velocity of the ball as it travelled around the circumference of the wheel, and the computer would then predict at what point the ball would fall into the rotor and whereabouts it was likely to come to rest. These predictions would be transmitted to the bettor by means of electronic signals, each of which would indicate a separate octant, or group of five numbers physically adjacent around the wheel. The bettor would then place betting chips on the five numbers indicated.

Bass described his emotions when he first operated the computer under laboratory conditions.

After a few false starts, I begin to get the rhythm. I learn not to hurry the clicks. I breathe easily and pace myself. I get better at deciphering solenoid buzzes and translating them into numbers. Standing under a bare light bulb, Doyne and I lean over the wheel for another hour. We listen to the ball rattle around the track and clatter down into the rotor's metal pockets. We're mesmerized, locked into the game so deeply that someone walking in on us might have thought he'd stumbled on the local numbers racket. This is my maiden voyage at the controls of the computer. I'm transported by the precision of the machine, the rhythm of the game, the whirl of numbers at the bottom of the varnished bowl, and the shine of the ball as its sails time and again for its rendezvous with destiny.

Rather than merely predicting the ball's trajectory, it feels as if I'm actually *steering* it. I can nudge the controls of the computer and bring the ball in for a perfect landing time and again on the surface of the spinning disk. I work the switches, and the ball drops from orbit to touch down dead-centre in the predicted octant of numbers coming around to meet it. It's as if I'm controlling the outcome of the game, nursing the little white ball by remote control through the Newtonian cosmos of a roulette wheel whose laws I've mastered.

However, although the Eudaemonic computer worked well under laboratory conditions, it failed to perform in the casinos. There were several reasons for this, of which the most important was that the noise emanating from the casinos' own electronics distorted the computer's signals, so the bettors were only sporadically able to follow its instructions.

This was, of course, a problem that William Nelson Darnborough never encountered. Since he was not reliant on high technology to formulate his predictions, he could not be disrupted by the malfunctions to which high technology is vulnerable. Darnborough's success, set against the failures of Dr Thorp and Eudaemonic Enterprises, demonstrates that the human brain is superior to any machine.

If there are those who are sceptical that such a feat could be accomplished, it may be worth citing evidence from the other side of the casino table. In *Loaded Dice*, John Soares, who was himself a casino dealer experienced in cheating honest gamblers out of their hard-earned money, wrote that

A good wheel man (croupier) knows how to spin the ball away from a heavy bettor. Certain numbers are grouped together on the wheel, so if the bettor has big money on these numbers the wheel man manipulates the ball so it lands in another section. A good wheel man develops a deft touch spinning the ball, and can amaze initiates with his accuracy. The same is true when a bettor is heavy on certain numbers that are clustered together. The wheel man can direct the ball away from that cluster. He never minds if the small bettors win, so long as he keeps the heavy bettors away from their colours and numbers. It is a good idea to avoid roulette wheels where the croupier does not give the ball a fast spin.

In other words, a skilful croupier can drop the roulette ball into certain sections of the wheel with the same accuracy as a top snooker player can cue balls into the pockets of a snooker table.

What Darnborough did was reverse the usual odds of the game by using the regularity of the croupier's spin to predict the sector of the wheel into which the ball would land. He may also have been assisted by casino procedures in Monte Carlo before the First World War. The pace of the game and the spin of the roulette wheel was far slower in Monte Carlo at the turn of the twentieth century than it is in contemporary British or American casinos. According to John Soares, it is easier to control and predict the destination of a roulette ball on a slowly spinning wheel.

If this hypothesis of Darnborough's success is correct, he deserved to win his fortune, since he must have been a man of exceptional abilities. He had the nerve which is the hallmark of all successful gamblers, and the supreme confidence to back his judgement with hard cash even after inevitable losing runs. Moreover, he was marked out by the sheer speed of his operations: of his eye, his brain, and his hand – honed by years of study and training.

His system must have worked as follows. First of all, he must have spent some time studying a particular roulette wheel and croupier before placing any bets. He would have avoided those croupiers who appeared erratic or volatile in their actions or who spun the wheel too rapidly. Having selected a suitable target, he would have had to watch very closely to see at what point on the roulette wheel the ball was launched; with what force the croupier impelled it; and how strongly the roulette rotor was spinning in the opposite direction. Assimilating all this information, Darnborough would then have used it to predict how many revolutions the roulette ball would travel before falling off the circumference of the wheel and into the rotor, and how far the ball would then bounce before coming to land on a single number. He would apply this prediction by placing bets on the consecutive numbers covering the segment of the wheel where he believed that the ball would land. In order to bet in such a way, he must have had an image of the roulette wheel constantly in his mind, so that he knew instantaneously and without conscious thought which numbers were adjacent to each other around the wheel.

All this he would do in a matter of a very few seconds, between the moment the ball left the croupier's hand and the moment the croupier called, '*Rien ne va plus.*' And he would have had to repeat the procedure over and over again during the course of a playing session, without tiring or erring, almost by instinct, so that, as the wheel spun its way hypnotically through an evening, Darnborough would cease to have any independent existence, but would become totally bound up in its motion, an adjunct to it, a human computer whose program and response was determined by it.

No, to be a successful gambler is not easy; and those few who win a fortune on the tables of the world's casinos must possess outstanding qualities to overcome the odds stacked against them.

Roulette Scams and the Laws
of Probability

For every individual like Jaggers or Darnborough who has won a fortune in the world's casinos, there are thousands who have lost a fortune.

Under normal circumstances, casino games cannot be consistently beaten by the player. This is because, unlike other forms of gambling such as horse racing or sports betting, casino games are purely mathematical in their conception. The casinos comprehend precisely the mathematics of the games they offer, and arrange them in such a way as to ensure that they enjoy an advantage over the players. The mathematical purity of the games constitute one of their great attractions to gamblers, yet it is precisely their mathematical laws that condemn the vast majority of those who play to ultimate defeat.

The scientific study of the laws governing games of chance is generally traced back to the day in 1654 when an aristocratic French gambler, the Chevalier de Méré, approached his friend Blaise Pascal with a problem. The Chevalier wanted to know why the odds of getting a 6 in four rolls of a die were greater than the odds of getting a double 6 in 24 rolls of two dice. By the Chevalier's reckoning, the odds should have been the same, since there are six possible outcomes of a roll of a single die, compared to 36 possible outcomes of a roll of two dice. He therefore believed that the probability of getting a double 6 with two dice should be $\frac{6}{36}$ or $\frac{1}{6}$.

This problem vexed the Chevalier because it was costing him a good deal of money. He had made a fair profit by offering even money against anyone willing to bet that he would not get a 6 in four rolls of a standard die. Most of the time he won, and as it became obvious to his victims that the odds were stacked against them their interest in the wager dwindled. Some punter then suggested that, in order to make the game more interesting, he should extend the game to two dice, and offer even money against getting a double 6 at least once in every 24 rolls. De Méré took up the challenge, but discovered to his consternation that he lost money on the bet. In a large number of trials, he found that he did not get a double 6 in 24 rolls more than 50 per cent of the time. In desperation, he turned to Pascal to try to discover the flaw in his reasoning.

Pascal approached the problem from another angle. Rather than calculating how many times de Méré could expect to roll a 6, he calculated how many times he would roll a number *other than* 6. He thus adopted the methodology of many successful bridge players, whose first question when looking at their hands is not how many tricks they will win, but how many tricks they are likely to lose, and whether there is any way those losses can be cut.

Clearly, the chance of not rolling a 6 on any roll of a single die is $\frac{5}{6}$, against a $\frac{1}{6}$ chance of rolling a 6. The sum of the two probabilities must always be 1 or 100 per cent: that is, it is certain that either a 6 or a number other than 6 must be rolled.

This much was self-evident. Pascal then went on to calculate the probability of not rolling a 6 on four rolls of a single die. If the chance of not rolling a 6 on one roll is $\frac{5}{6}$, the chance of not rolling a 6 on four rolls is $\frac{5}{6} \times \frac{5}{6} \times \frac{5}{6} \times \frac{5}{6}$, or 0.48225 approximately. Thus, de Méré would fail to roll a 6 approximately 48 per cent of the time, and would succeed approximately 52 per cent of the time. Of every 100 bets placed, de Méré would therefore win just over half. This theoretical result confirmed de Méré's practical experience.

Pascal then went on to examine the chances of rolling a double 6 in 24 rolls of two dice. In a single trial, the chance of failure was $\frac{35}{36}$. In 24 trials, the chance of failure would therefore be $\frac{35}{36}$ multiplied by itself 24 times, which gives a result of 0.508596. That is, the Chevalier de Méré would fail to roll a double 6 in 24 trials approximately 50.9 per cent of the time, and would succeed in doing so 49.1 per cent of the time. Thus, by offering even money to anyone willing to bet that he would not roll a double 6, he stood to lose approximately (50.9–49.1) out of every 100 units bet, or 1.8 per cent of the total money wagered. From the Chevalier's point of view, it was a losing proposition.

The problem illustrates three important principles. First, there is a very narrow margin between success and failure in games of chance, and even the narrowest of margins is likely to prove decisive in the long run. Second, intuition can be misleading: de Méré's reasoning on the probabilities of rolling a double 6 appears superficially correct but is in fact wrong. And third, a wise gambler who finds things are not running according to plan should not throw good money after bad, but should rather pause and take stock, as the Chevalier de Méré did. An examination of the assumptions on which the strategy is based may well reveal some overlooked flaw.

The Chevalier de Méré had the good fortune of being able to turn to one of the greatest mathematicians of the age for advice. By doing so, he stimulated research which provided the basis of modern science, since it led to the development of a rigorous theory of probability and statistics.

Blaise Pascal has given his name to the English language as the man who laid Pascal's Wager, a bet on the existence of God. We should believe in God, argued Pascal, because if He exists, then following His commandments will save us from eternal perdition; while if He does not exist, it makes no difference whether we believe in Him or not. Pascal's Wager was the original shot to nothing.

Pascal's lasting fame lies in the contributions he made to mathematics, particularly geometry and probability theory. Spurred on by the gambling problems posed by de Méré, Pascal entered into a correspondence with another great mathematician, Pierre de Fermat, and in an exchange of half a dozen letters they established the foundations of a scientific methodology that has endured to today. We may wonder why such great intellects as Pascal and Fermat expended so much effort on what appear to be trivial games of chance. The answer is that such games constitute closed systems which provide perfectly controlled conditions for testing different hypotheses. As a contemporary of Pascal, the Dutch physicist Christiaan Huygens, wrote in his work *On Calculations in Games of Chance*, 'The reader will note that we are dealing not only with games, but also that the foundations of a very interesting and profound theory are being laid.'

Pascal introduced the principle of mathematical induction whereby what holds for a series of numbers in specific cases may be deduced to hold in all cases. This principle is immensely powerful, since it implies that results obtained in controlled conditions can be extended to problems pertaining outside those conditions. Pascal realized that games of chance provided ideal conditions for setting up and testing hypotheses that have broader applications in the real world.

However the relationship is symbiotic. Just as the principles of probability were first tested in games of chance, so the gambler must adopt a scientific approach if he or she is to achieve success. The tiny minority of gamblers who actually make money from gambling use the laws of probability to assist them in their endeavours. Thus, the professional gambler does not ask, 'Will this bet win?' but rather, 'What are the true odds of this bet winning, and do they exceed the odds being offered?'

In order to analyse casino games scientifically, it is necessary to appreciate the properties which generate their results. Roulette and dice games are examples of Bernoulli systems. These systems were first defined by the Swiss mathematician Jakob Bernoulli in his posthumously published work *Ars Conjectandi* (1713) as having three properties.

First, the possible results of each play are *mutually exclusive*. In roulette, the ball may land on a red or a black number in any spin, but not on both. In a dice game, the die may land on any number between 1 and 6, but not on more than one number in any roll.

Second, the results of a series of plays are *independent* from one play to another. The result of one spin of the roulette wheel has no bearing on the result of any later spin; nor does the outcome of any roll of the dice affect the outcome of any subsequent roll. The dice have no memory.

Third, the probability of any result is *constant* from one play to the next. In the case of an unbiased roulette wheel with a single zero, the probability that the ball will land on a red or black number is always $\frac{18}{37}$, or approximately 48.65 per cent, irrespective of the sequence of numbers that has occurred previously. Similarly, the probability that a die will land on any number between 1 and 6 is always $\frac{1}{6}$, or approximately 16.66 per cent, provided the die is evenly balanced.

A further implied property of roulette and dice games offered in casinos is that the probability of any result on which equivalent odds are offered by the house is equal. For example, in roulette, the chance of any number from zero to 36 coming up is exactly the same, at 36–1 against, for a pay-off of 35–1.

Jaggers and Darnborough succeeded in beating the game of roulette only by cracking the carefully constructed Bernoulli system. Jaggers identified biased wheels which tilted the odds in favour of certain numbers and against others. The bias on the wheel meant that the true probability of the roulette ball landing on certain numbers was greater than 36–1. Since the house offered fixed odds of 35–1 against every number, Jaggers could exploit the tilt by backing the favoured numbers.

A similar result was obtained by cruder methods by John Soares and his associates in the dice games offered by Nevada casinos during the 1960s and 1970s. As Soares describes it in *Loaded Dice*, they simply substituted loaded dice for the casino's own fair dice, and then betted heavily on the numbers most likely to come up.

Darnborough's system involved identifying a relationship between successive spins of the roulette wheel. The regularity of the croupier's spin implied that the second property of a Bernoulli system did not hold because the results of different spins were not truly independent of one another.

If there is no relationship between successive spins, then one of the most important results derived by Jakob Bernoulli ensures that the gambler will lose in the long run. The result is the Bernoulli theorem, or the law of large numbers, which states that the larger the number of trials within a Bernoulli system, the more likely it is that the actual results of the trials will approximate their mathematical expectation.

This is an extremely powerful result. It is the foundation upon which the wealth of the world's casinos is built. It implies that, no matter how the results fluctuate in the short term, a casino can ultimately be certain of winning the difference between the odds it offers and the true mathematical odds of a game.

Where this does not appear to be happening, and it appears that a gambler is winning consistently against the odds, suspicions will be aroused that all is not as it should be.

One such incident was reported at the Golden Horseshoe Casino in London's Queensway in June, 1991. According to the London *Evening Standard* of 20 June 1991, a mystery lady entered the casino one evening and over the course of the next few hours proceeded to win almost £750,000. Her winning system involved betting £100 chips on the same series of numbers on a single roulette wheel in the casino. Those numbers came up with remarkable consistency:

Casino staff watched with amazement and growing suspicion as her fortune increased. She was unknown to them and appeared to be unescorted ... As she was walking out of the Golden Horseshoe Casino with her winnings, written out on a fistful of £50,000 cheques, staff were waiting to take the roulette wheel apart to see if it had been tampered with. They found that the delicate tensioner screws holding the numbers ring in place had been adjusted in such a way as to make it more likely for the numbers the woman had been betting on to come up.

The company hopes to draw a discreet veil over the incident, but Henry Robinson, spokesman for the casino owners, said, 'There was something wrong with the wheel and we couldn't stop the game while it was in progress.' Alan

Bobroff, casino director, added, 'Our own security staff and management acted very promptly and efficiently to avoid a major loss.'

Despite the quoted comments of Messrs Robinson and Bobroff, the suspicion remains that the scam might have gone undetected had the cheats been less greedy. If they had been prepared to settle for a few thousand pounds, rather than seeking to win the best part of a million, the wheel might not have been so thoroughly checked after the casino closed, and the casino's management might have accepted their loss as a normal statistical swing. As it was, the scam was so blatant that it clearly fell outside the norms of probability and was bound to alert the casino to the possibility of fraud.

The Golden Horseshoe scam was a dishonest variant of the Jaggers method for beating roulette. While William Jaggers and his assistants recorded several hundred thousand spins of the Monte Carlo roulette wheels in order to identify significant biases, the mystery lady and her accomplices simply fixed the Horseshoe's wheel before play began. Safe in the knowledge that the wheel was already biased, they proceeded to clean up.

A dishonest variant of the Darnborough method for beating roulette was reported at the Palm Beach Club in Mayfair in the late 1980s. According to my hypothesis, Darnborough beat the wheel by using his powers of observation and lightning reflexes to predict where the roulette ball was likely to land in time to place bets on the winning segment. But why go to all this trouble if you could be absolutely certain of the number on which the ball would land *before it even left the croupier's hand?*

It would seem that we are leaving the world of probabilities, and entering a universe of necromancy. Surely it is impossible to predict the exact landing place of a roulette ball by scientific means, given the randomness imparted by the frets and vanes around the wheel. Yet this was precisely what one player apparently achieved one evening at the Palm Beach. Spin after spin, he would toss large denomination chips to the croupier as he shouted the numbers he wished to back. The croupier would then place the chips on the required numbers and, amazingly, after the ball had landed one of the lucky gambler's chips would always be found on the winning number.

Note that these coups occurred under the scrutiny of a video camera. As the gambler's winnings mounted, the interest of the security room focused on the table where he was playing; yet the security men could discern nothing untoward about his activities. Spin after spin, he just seemed to have an uncanny knack of backing winning numbers. Backing five or six numbers on each spin, he would reap a pay-off of 35–1 on the winner for a 700 per cent profit. With the wheel spinning thirty times an hour, it would not be long before he busted the casino.

The gambler's undoing was that he pushed his luck too far. For the first few coups, the security men did not even notice him among the bubbling crowds milling around the casino. For the next few coups, they observed with interest as he enjoyed an apparent lucky streak and his chips built up to impressive proportions. Had he been wise, the gambler would have got out while he was ahead with a few thousand pounds. But he kept on playing so long that it was obvious his winning streak was not due to luck, but to something else.

As casino executives observed the action with increasing alarm, they noticed something curious about the coup on the roulette table. Although the gambler passed a number of chips to the croupier which were then placed on several numbers as the wheel was spinning, the croupier never seemed to have time to place all the chips before the ball landed. Furthermore the chip which covered the winning number frequently appeared to be the last one placed.

The truth became apparent. It was not difficult for the gambler to predict the winning number – because the ball had already landed on it! The gambler was in a conspiracy with the croupier and the inspector supervising the game to defraud the casino. He would shout a series of numbers to the croupier while the ball was in motion, and the croupier would then place the chips on all the requested numbers apart from one. As the ball landed, the croupier would glance at the wheel and then place the final chips on the winning number. As it was all done by word of mouth according to correct casino procedures, there was no way that visual security surveillance could prove that anything dishonest had occurred. The other players at the table would be too concerned with their own bets to notice that the croupier was placing one of the high roller's bets on a number other than those he had specified.

The fraud was detected only because the gambler's streak was so extremely improbable. Again, it might have worked if the three-man team of the gambler, croupier and inspector had been a little less greedy. Although casino managements accept that some roulette players win in the short term, if a gambler appears to defy the odds over a long period, casino executives will want to know why. Unlike the more gullible members of the gambling public, they are sceptical about tales of amazing runs of luck. They believe only in the harsh logic of the laws of probability. Where someone appears to be winning in defiance of those laws, they will suspect fraud.

They are usually right.

The Coup of the Prince of Canino

Albert Einstein once observed that single-zero roulette could only be beaten by a gambler with infinite capital playing in a game without limits for eternity. In all other cases, the mathematical edge enjoyed by the house would grind down any player over a long enough series of trials.

There are at least three other methods that gamblers have successfully employed to beat the wheel. The first is by physically fixing the wheel before the game commences as in the Golden Horseshoe scam, or interfering with the bets placed during the game as in the Palm Beach scam. If he were still with us, Professor Einstein would doubtless object that these methods do not constitute a valid refutation of his general point since they involve cheating.

However, there are two other methods that involve no physical interference with the game or the betting chips. The first involves predicting where the ball is likely to land – either by observation, as in Darnborough's case, or with the assistance of computer technology as attempted by Eudaemonic Enterprises. The second entails identifying biases in the roulette wheel, as William Jaggers and the Hibbs-Walford team succeeded in doing.

The application of these methods is not easy, and requires much concentrated effort. I am not aware of any case where they have been applied in contemporary British casinos. Even if a gambler mastered the Jaggers or Hibbs-Walford techniques for identifying biases, anyone sitting down for several hours and recording roulette results without betting would soon raise the suspicions of casino executives, and probably be barred. Furthermore, to be reasonably certain that a bias did exist, results would have to be recorded over several days' play, and this would carry the risk that the wheel was replaced or rebalanced between sessions.

The only method I can think of that might beat the wheel would be as follows. A small team of gamblers might be formed, to operate in shifts in a casino such as the Golden Nugget in Shaftesbury Avenue. This casino has about a dozen roulette wheels whose results are electronically recorded on a scoreboard above the casino entrance. At 2 p.m. when the casino opens, the first two team members would enter and sit at different tables. They would each have the responsibility for recording the results of half-a-dozen roulette wheels. As cover, they would place £5 bets on even-money chances in order to appear as normal gamblers. After three quarters of an hour, two more team members would enter the casino and the original two would cash in and leave. This process would go on until midnight. Outside the casino, the results would be analysed, probably with the aid of a computer, in the team's headquarters.

Between midnight and 2 a.m. a final analysis would be undertaken of the results, and an assessment made of whether any of the wheels had a statistical bias. If they did, a team member who had not previously entered the casino would go in with a substantial bankroll, act like a drunken late-night high roller, and proceed to cover the segment favoured by the bias with very large bets up to the table maximum.

I offer this system free of charge with the following wealth warnings.

First, its excution requires a well-organized, disciplined, trained team capable of recording the results absolutely accurately without arousing casino suspicion.

Second, over the twelve hours between 2 p.m. and 2 a.m. each wheel might be spun approximately 600 times. This is not a sufficiently large sample to identify bias with any great confidence. As approximate orders of magnitude, any octant (or group of five consecutive numbers around the roulette wheel) would be expected to come up 80 times in 600 spins of the wheel. For two-thirds of the time, the ball should land on each octant on between 70 and 90 occasions out of each 600 trials. Extreme deviation from these limits may indicate bias. For example, if an octant came up more than 105 times in a series of 600 trials, it might be because the wheel was slightly tilted. Alternatively, it might merely be a 1-in-800 chance. Similarly if a sector came up less than 55 times, it might be the result of bias in the wheel or a 1-in-235 chance. If these extreme deviations are the result of chance, there would be no reason for the pattern to continue when the high roller placed his bets. The only way round this would be to record the results over several days, and pray that the wheels were not changed during that period.

A third problem with the system is that anyone seeking to use statistical methods to identify biases in a roulette wheel should bear in mind that the casinios would be likely to bar any individual or team they suspected of executing such a coup.

Given all these difficulties, what are the chances of beating roulette over a short period? Even if we agree with Einstein that, over a long enough period, the odds will grind down the players and ensure a win for the house, we also know that most social gamblers will only play for a short period. In the course of an evening's entertainment, a gambler may only place a couple of hundred bets. Over that period, the gambler may lose his or her entire stake – or may double or triple it. The interesting question is therefore not what will happen over the long run but rather how the results will fluctuate in the short run for a single individual placing a small number of bets to which the harsh logic of the law of large numbers does not apply.

The answer to this question was provided in the eighteenth century by one of the intellectual heirs of Pascal and Bernoulli, a French exile named Abraham de Moivre. De Moivre was a Huguenot who spent two years of his early life imprisoned in France because of his religious beliefs. On his release from prison in 1688 he fled to London, where he pursued his career as a mathematician. He was elected to the Royal Society at the age of thirty in 1697. De Moivre passed much of his life in exile playing cards and dice in the coffee houses of Covent Garden during the intervals between giving tutorials on mathematics at Slaughter's Coffee House in St Martin's Lane. He studied the works of Pascal, Montmort and Bernoulli, and sought to extend their ideas on the mathematics of games. On the basis of his research and his own experiences as a gambler, he wrote the *Doctrine of Chances*, which extended the theory of dice permutations and the analysis of card games.

It may have been during the long hours he spent gambling in London's coffee houses that de Moivre had a flash of brilliance that was to form his most significant contribution to mathematical science. He realized that, as play goes on, the actual results fluctuate from the mathematically expected result. However, the degree of fluctuation does not vary with the number of plays, but rather with the square root of the number of plays.

Thus, if a gambler places 100 bets of one unit each on an even-money chance in single-zero roulette, such as a red number, he or she expects to lose an average 1.35 units out of the 100 units wagered. For two-thirds of the time, the actual result will lie between −6.18 units lost and +3.48 units won, a two standard deviation of approximately 10 per cent of the units bet. Over 1,000 spins, the standard deviation is proportionately less than over 100 trials: for two-thirds of the time, the actual result will lie between −29 units lost and +2 units won, a range of approximately 3 per cent of the 1,000 units bet. Over 10,000 spins, the acutal result will lie between −183 units lost and −86 units lost for two-thirds of the time – a two standard deviation spread which represents approximately 1 per cent of the 10,000 units bet.

The principles of standard deviation are explained in greater detail in Appendix 1. The point to note here is that, as play goes on, so the degree of fluctuation tends to diminish. The reason is that the random factors impacting on the results of a game tend to cancel each other out as the number of plays increases.

De Moivre's theorem thus provides the missing link between the apparently wild and random fluctuations that may be experienced in the short term, and Bernoulli's law of large numbers that applies in the long term. This enables us to predict what will happen in the course of a game of roulette or dice with unambiguous precision.

What will happen is that, as the number of trials increases, the absolute value of the deviation of the actual from the expected result will increase, but the percentage deviation will decrease. Actual results will fluctuate wildly over a few hundred trials, but the more trials that take place, the more likely it is that the fluctuations will tend to cancel each other out. In simple English, runs of bad luck and good luck are equally likely. Consequently, as the number of trials increases, so the aggregation of the actual results in roulette and dice games will tend to converge towards their mathematical expectation.

The implication is that a gambler may beat the roulette wheel over a few hundred spins, but as the number of spins of the wheel increases, so the percentages will grind him down into a loser. The longer play goes on, the greater the losses that will accumulate. In the example cited above, note that over 100 spins of the wheel the gambler backing even-money chances has a chance of approximately 36.5 per cent of coming out ahead. However, over 10,000 spins of the wheel the gambler's chance of winning is less than one in twenty.

De Moivre's theorem does provide some clues as to why, despite this fact, roulette remains the most popular casino game in Europe. First of all, while it may be mathematically impossible for the player to beat the game consistently, there is a reasonable chance of coming out ahead in the short term. The house edge of 1.35 per cent on even-money bets and 2.7 per cent on numbers or permutations of numbers is decisive over the long run, but small enough to offer the gambler a reasonable chance of success in the short run. This is not true of American roulette, where the presence of a double zero on the wheel implies that the house edge is 5.3 per cent on individual numbers – a fact which goes a long way to explaining why roulette is much less popular in the United States than in Europe.

A second reason for the popularity of European roulette is that the range of bets offered can appeal to all gambling temperaments, from the risk-averse grinder who aims for a modest profit on even-money wagers to the long-shot speculator who stakes on the numbers in the hope of a 35–1 pay-off.

A third attraction lies in the sheer speed of the game. In the time that it would take to resolve a horse race, a roulette wheel will have spun twenty or thirty times.

Finally, the intrinsic mathematical purity of the game has drawn system players to it ever since the Renaissance.

This combination of factors has made roulette the most popular casino game in Britain and continental Europe. The casinos themselves add to the mix by publicizing stories about the men and women who parlayed small stakes into fortunes on the roulette tables, like the man who broke the bank at Monte Carlo:

> As I walk along the Bois de Boulogne
> With an independent air
> You can hear the girls declare
> He must be a millionaire!
> You can hear them sigh and wish to die,
> You can see them wink a hopeful eye
> At the man who broke the bank at Monte Carlo!

What the casinos fail to mention in their promotional literature is that the man who broke the bank at Monte Carlo, William Jaggers, did not do so as a result of an amazing run of luck, but through his scientific analysis of biases on the roulette wheel.

The fact is that no system for playing or betting has been devised, or could ever be devised, to overcome the player's negative mathematical expectation on an unbiased roulette wheel where the ball is spun at random. The most a player can hope for in playing roulette (or in playing casino dice games, where the same principles apply) is to select the least worse bet, which is that bet where the player's expected losses are minimized.

It may come as a surprise to the social gambler to learn that the bets placed in casino games have different expectations of success. It is certainly true in dice games and the card game of punto banco, but it is also true in roulette.

The best bets in roulette are the even-money bets paying off 1 unit for each unit wagered: red or black, odd or even, high or low numbers. All other bets offer inferior odds for the player. The reason lies in the treatment of the zero. If the ball lands on the zero, all bets on individual numbers other than zero are lost. However, bets on red or black, odd or even, or high or low are placed *en prison*, and if the bet wins on the next spin the wager is returned. The probability of saving a bet placed *en prison* is thus 50 per cent. Because of the favourable treatment of even-money bets, the expected loss on them is only half as great as that on individual numbers. Or, to be more optimistic, it is twice as likely that a gambler will enjoy a lucky winning streak backing even-money chances as backing individual numbers. Even a gambler playing with speculative money that he is willing to risk for the chance of a big return would be well advised to back the even-money chances.

One gambler who recognized this was Charles Lucien Bonaparte, Prince of Canino, who descended on the Kursaal casino in the central European spa town of Homburg in September 1852.

The Prince was a nephew of the Emperor Napoleon. After Napoleon's death in 1815, the young Charles Lucien was taken to the United States by Napoleon's elder brother Joseph, the deposed King of Spain. They lived in exile on an estate at Point Breeze near Bordertown in New Jersey. Lucien developed an interest in ornithology and spent much of his time observing bird life in the forests of New Jersey and neighbouring states. In 1828 he published an authoritative work on the subject entitled *The Genera of North American Birds*. He also developed a consuming interest in members of the opposite sex.

Meanwhile, back in Europe, the fortunes of the Bonaparte family were on the rise once more. Following the revolutions of 1848, Charles Lucien's first cousin Louis Napoleon restored the Napoleonic Empire in France. In his account of Charles Lucien's career in *Gamblers of Yesteryear*, Russell T. Barnhart writes,

In politics, Charles Lucien Bonaparte, the second Prince of Canino, became a radical and an enemy of Pope Pius IX. When the latter fled Rome to sanctuary in the Kingdom of Naples during the Revolution of 1848, the Prince of Canino was elected vice president of the radical Roman popular assembly and even signed the proclamation calling the people to arms . . .

Although revolting against popes was a far cry from noting the flights of birds, the Prince of Canino was allowed to return to Paris a few months before his cousin, Napoleon III, ascended the throne of France. In Paris the Prince of Canino devoted himself to his three favourite pursuits – radicalism, lechery and ornithology – which endeared him to nobody but ornithologists.

With his cousin installed as Emperor of the French, fortune seemed to be favouring the Prince of Canino. Perhaps feeling that he was on a roll, he decided to try his luck in the Homburg Kursaal in the autumn of 1852. The Kursaal was run by the twin brothers François and Louis Blanc, who attracted gamblers by the same method employed a century and a half later by the Binion family in Las Vegas – they offered value for money in the form of the best odds gamblers could get anywhere. In particular, they offered a roulette game with a single zero on the wheel, rather than a double zero as was offered by other European casinos at the time, thus halving the house's *refait*, or mathematical edge, over the gambler.

The Prince of Canino was among those attracted by the small house edge offered at the Kursaal. Contemporary mathematicians have established that a gambler's best hope of success in any game where the odds are against him lies in adopting a strategy of maximum boldness supported with a heavy bankroll. In other words, if your bankroll is large relative to that of the casino, and you bet aggressively for a short period – and get out after that period – then you have a reasonable chance of finishing ahead. By contrast, a gambler with a small bankroll betting small amounts over a long period is mathematically virtually certain to be ruined.

The Prince of Canino adopted the strategy of maximum boldness. It is probable that he had more funds at his disposal than the Blanc brothers, and as events transpired he also had luck on his side. In *Der Zauberer von Homburg und Monte Carlo*, Count Egon Corti recounted the tale.

The players crowded around the stout, bull-necked prince with his dark, flashing eyes. On the table before him lay piles of gold, and from the first his stakes were the highest allowed by the bank. Changing from the roulette table to trente-et-quarante, he won almost without a break and with incredible luck, retrieving his few losses by staking on the even-money chances. In only four days from September 26th to September 29th he won 83,700 florins, and the bank was constantly compelled to replenish its supplies of money at the tables where the prince happened to be playing.

These huge and repeated winnings alarmed the authorities of the casino, who foresaw that, should the prince's luck continue, the bank's entire reserves of 300,000 florins would be exhausted and play would have to be stopped. On the evening of the 29th it came to an end when the prince had exhausted the reserves at both tables.

At his wit's end, the manager hurried to the Rothschilds in Frankfurt and asked for an advance of 200,000 florins on the 400 shares belonging to the company. But Baron Rothschild refused to make any advance before having received telegraphic instructions from Paris, for he was aware that Francois Blanc possessed a large private fortune.

On 2 October, the prince reappeared at the Kursaal and lost heavily. It seemed that the danger had passed. But his own enormous fortune enabled him to withstand these losses and late in the evening his luck turned.

Count Corti recounts what happened next.

Though the bank's reserves had been strongly reinforced, he won so heavily that on retiring to his hotel that evening he took away with him no less than 260,400 florins.

The management immediately called a meeting of all the company's stock-holders present in Homburg to decide what measures should be taken to avert a catastrophe.

It was agreed that the maximum stake on the even-money chances should be reduced from 4,000 florins to 2,000 and that the landgrave's government should be asked permission to introduce the double refait at trente-et-quarante and the second zero at roulette. Meanwhile a telegram had arrived from François Blanc, placing 120,000 florins at the disposal of the company.

It was a classic casino response to the threat posed by a well-heeled gambler on a run of luck. Increase the resources you have available, reduce the table maximum, and enhance the house's edge – then wait for the law of large numbers to grind down the high roller.

It did not, however, succeed in grinding down the Prince of Canino. Whether he had got wind of the imminent rule changes, or whether he simply wished to pursue other pleasures elsewhere (which could have been bad news for the maidens of Paris), we do not know. All that is recorded is that on the morning of 3 October 1852, Charles Lucien

Bonaparte departed from Homburg, taking 352,380 of the Kursaal's florins with him.

This was probably the nearest the Kursaal came to bankruptcy. It set the casino's development plans back by several years, as the decision was taken to defer the Kursaal's enlargement and the construction of a new hotel until the casino's working capital was increased by another 200,000 florins.

But even at this low point in his fortunes, François Blanc's nerve held and his belief that the laws of probability would prevail against even the luckiest gambler remained undimmed.

While all Homburg was in a flutter of alarm lest another another such successful gambler appear, François Blanc was comparatively calm. He had often maintained that none but a really big gambler was formidable to the bank, and even then only if he commanded a capital very much larger than that of the bank. He was sufficiently optimistic to regret Prince Charles Lucien's departure, for he felt sure that in the long run the prince would have lost back every whit of his winnings.

Blanc was confident that the Prince of Canino would return some day, for experience told him that nothing encourages people to go on gambling more than a good big run of luck and the mirage of boundless wealth it creates.

Der Zauberer von Homburg und Monte Carlo

While François Blanc's analysis was right in every other respect, his prediction that the Prince of Canino would return to Homburg proved to be wrong. Charles Lucien Bonaparte died at the age of 54 on 31 July 1857 without ever having surrendered his winnings back to the Kursaal. His remains one of the few attested cases of a gambler who won a fortune against the odds at roulette. He was shrewd enough to quit before a short-term fluctuation in his favour was ground down into an inevitable long-term loss. And having won once, he wisely never gambled again.

High Rollers at Homburg

Over the years, many gamblers have dreamed of emulating Charles Lucien Bonaparte by devising some betting system that would take advantage of short-term fluctuations in the game of roulette and enable them to walk away from the tables with a fortune.

One of the most famous dreamers was the Countess Sophie Kisseleff, immortalized in the character of Grandmamma in Dostoevsky's *The Gambler*. The Countess was an inveterate gambler who dissipated a fortune on the roulette tables of nineteenth-century Europe. Her first recorded visit to the Homburg Kursaal was in 1852, the year that Charles Lucien Bonaparte almost bankrupted it. She no doubt earned the undying gratitude of François Blanc by helping to restore his fortunes after the severe dent they had received at the hands of the Prince of Canino.

In *Les Tripots d'Allemagne*, Alfred Sirven related that

Countess Kisseleff's favourite game is roulette, which she doesn't leave for days on end, covering with florins, like a crazy woman, almost all the numbers and losing without cessation. During her annual stay in Homburg she loses on an average 500,000 florins. One season she was forced to sell even her carriage and her horses.

A very pious soul, Countess Kisseleff, after three years of enormous losses, decided to go to Rome to ask Pope Pius IX for absolution. His Holiness accorded it to her but made her swear renunciation of gambling at Homburg. But passion moved her more than religion.

She returned to Homburg, and do you know how she attenuated her perjury? 'I shall play no longer for my own account,' she announced, 'but rather for that of the poor, to whom I shall donate all my winnings.' Oh, Charity, what is not committed in thy name?

From this account, three reasons already emerge as to why the Countess failed to repeat the coup of the Prince of Canino. First, she bet on the numbers rather than the even-money chances – so the edge she had to overcome was twice as great as that which faced the prince. Second, she spread her bets over a wide range of numbers, rather than concentrating them as is recommended by the strategy of maximum boldness. Third, and fatally, she played 'without cessation', rather than setting a definite time limit and quitting once that time was up, win or lose. These factors made it virtually certain that the Countess would fall victim to the law of large numbers.

Yet there was a certain warped logic to her play, as Dostoevsky describes. In *The Gambler*, Grandmamma joins a party of Russian and French gamblers in the town of Roulettenburg, and is tempted into the casino there to watch the gamblers at play. At first, she is curious only about the personalities and motivation of the players. Little by little, her attention shifts to the game of roulette on which they are gambling.

As well as I could, I explained to Grandmamma the meaning of the numerous combinations of *rouge et noir, pair et impair, manque et passe*, and finally the ins and outs of staking on the numbers. Grandmamma listened carefully, remembered, asked questions, and learned bits by heart . . .

'And what is zero? That croupier there with curly hair, the head one, called out zero just now. And why did he rake in everything that was anywhere on the table? Such a heap; why did he take it all for himself? What does it mean?'

'Zero means that the bank wins, Grandmamma. If the little ball falls into zero, whatever has been staked goes to the bank. It's true there is one coup which neither wins nor loses, but the bank doesn't pay anything out.'

'Well, well! And I don't get anything?'

'Yes, Grandmamma, if you have staked on zero, you get paid thirty-five times as much when zero comes up.'

Thus apprised, Grandmamma makes her fatal first bet, on the zero. Worse is to follow, for the zero comes up and puts Grandmamma into a comfortable profit. As François Blanc observed, there is nothing that encourages people to go on gambling more than a run of luck and the mirage of boundless wealth it creates. So it is with Grandmamma, who is now hooked by her own flawed logic. Grandmamma's reasoning is that it is the presence of the zero that provides the house with its edge. It is therefore in the house's interest that the roulette ball lands on the zero. Since the house always wins, any gambler who bets with the house by backing the zero will also win.

'Again, again, again! Stake again!' cried Grandmamma. I raised no more objections but shrugged my shoulders and staked a further twelve friedrichs d'or. The wheel spun for a long time. Grandmamma positively quivered as she followed it with her eyes. 'Can she really believe that she will win again on zero?' I wondered, looking at her with astonishment. A definite conviction that she would win shone in her face, an unshakeable expectation that at any moment would come the call of zero. The ball dropped into the compartment.

'Zero!' called the croupier.

'Well!' Grandmamma turned to me with a flourish of triumph.

I was a gambler myself; I realized it at that moment. My arms and legs were trembling and my head throbbed. It was, of course, a rare happening for zero to come up three times out of some ten or so; but there was nothing particularly astonishing about it. I had myself seen zero turn up three times running two days before, and on that occasion one of the players, zealously recording all the coups on a piece of paper, had remarked aloud that no earlier than the previous day that same zero had come out exactly once in twenty-four hours.

Grandmamma is deaf to the suggestion that her win is due to nothing more than standard deviation. After her initial triumph, luck inevitably begins to turn against Grandmamma; but it is too late. Her interest in the game has grown into a fully-fledged obsession and she dissipates ever-increasing quantities of her personal capital on the roulette tables.

Like the real-life Countess Kisseleff, her remorse leads her to vow to play for charity rather than herself.

'Today I lost fifteen thousand roubles at your double-damned roulette. Five years ago I promised to rebuild a wooden church on my estate near Moscow in stone, and instead I've thrown the lot away here. Now, my dear, I'm going to build the church.'

But if Grandmamma hopes that such sentiments will provoke divine intervention in her favour, she is to be sorely disappointed. The end is not long in coming.

The next day she lost everything she had in the world. It was bound to happen: for anybody of her kind, once started on that path, it is like sliding down a toboggan-run on a sledge, going faster and faster all the time. She played all day, until eight o'clock in the evening; I was not present, and only know what I have been told.

Potapych kept watch beside her at the station all day ... According to Potapych's reckoning, Grandmamma had lost altogether something like ninety thousand roubles that day, on top of her losses of the previous day. All her securities – five per cent bills, government loans, and all the stocks she had with her, had been changed, one after another. I wondered how she could have endured it for six or seven hours, sitting in her chair and hardly leaving the table, but Potapych told me that on one or two occasions she really began winning considerable sums; and then, carried away by the renewal of hope, she was quite unable to leave. Gamblers know how a man can sit in one place for almost twenty-four hours, playing cards and never turning his eyes to the right or the left.

While the Countess Kisseleff did more than her fair share to restore the Kursaal's fortunes after the coup of the Prince of Canino, there was no shortage of other willing volunteers eager to try their luck. Poets and politicians, millionaires, monarchs and mountebanks all converged on Homburg during its golden age. Among those who played roulette at the Kursaal was Dostoevsky himself, who was reduced to penury by his compulsion to gamble. Another visitor was the Spanish millionaire and 'professional' roulette player Thomas Garcia who, after defying the odds for an unusually long period during the mid-nineteenth century, finally lost his entire fortune at Homburg and died in poverty in a Trappist monastery.

Another adventurer who travelled to Homburg in search of a fortune was the English writer and journalist George Augustus Sala. He visited the town in 1858 with his friends Henry Vitzelly and Augustus Mayhew. In his *Life and Adventures*, Sala informs us that

Vitzelly had an 'infallible system' – the most infallible system that was ever known for winning at roulette – and we bound ourselves by a solemn league and covenant not to play any but this same infallible system.

Our system had nothing to do with the numbers on the roulette table; we were to break the bank by the following delightful means. If a colour, or odd or even, or over or under 18 won twice in a row, we were to bet against it; doubling our stakes if we lost and continuing to double our stakes till we won.

Vitzelly's system was in fact a crude variation of the martingale or doubling-up progression. The system requires the gambler to double his bet on an even-money chance after a loss, until ultimately it wins and the gambler gains a net amount equal to his original stake. This system, like many other popular betting progressions, possesses the insidious feature of appearing to offer the prospect of a secure profit with little risk. A naïve gambler could easily gain a misplaced confidence in such a system by winning small amounts in a number of sessions, before experiencing an ultimately certain large loss.

For example, suppose a gambler has £750 and decides to use the martingale system to generate a profit sufficient to pay for a good restaurant dinner one evening. He enters a casino, and proceeds to back an even-money chance on the roulette wheel. His first bet is £50, and he will then progress to £100, £200 and finally £400. His £750 bank gives him four chances to win a net amount of £50 and walk away with the profit he needs for an evening out. The chances are that he will succeed in achieving his target. Applying the methodology of Blaise Pascal, we can calculate the probability of failure as $\frac{19}{37} \times \frac{19}{37} \times \frac{19}{37} \times \frac{19}{37}$, or approximately 6.95 per cent. Our gambler will therefore enjoy a 'free' dinner more than nine times out of ten when he uses this system.

The snag is, of course, that sooner or later the even-money chance he is backing will *not* come up in four spins of the wheel, and not only will the gambler not enjoy a free dinner, but he will have lost £750 of his own capital to boot. It will be noted that the gambler would need fifteen winning sessions, making £50 on each occasion, in order to double his £750 capital, while he need only experience one losing session in order to lose it entirely. With a chance of failure of 6.95 per cent, the odds are that he will lose, on average, once in every 14.4 sessions (= $\frac{100}{6.95}$), thus ensuring that the casino comes out ahead in the long run.

However, Sala and his friends were not interested in the long run. At least they did not make the same mistake as the Countess Kisseleff of doubling the odds against them by backing individual numbers rather than even-money chances. And they were chancing their luck in beautiful surroundings.

We had travelled to Homburg via Rotterdam, Cologne, the Rhine river, and Frankfurt on the Main, and enjoyed ourselves hugely ... The weather at Homburg was unusually cold and became chillier as the evening drew in. The sun set in an agitated sea of clouds. The Taunus Mountains were a mass of deep blue, against which the white walls of the landgrave's castle stood out in full relief.

Homburg seemed to be overflowing with life. A perfect crowd alighted from the railway train. Droskies rattled along Louisstrasse. The Kursaal was ablaze with light. Stylishly-dressed men and women in evening and lounging costume paced the long corridor or flitted through the anterooms. The concert hall was three parts filled.

The gaming salons had their full complement of players. There were the same calculating old fogies, the same supercilious-looking young men, the same young girls and full-blown women with a nervous quivering about the lips, the same old sinners of both sexes whom one has known at these places the last ten or fifteen years.

Sala, *Life and Adventures*

The major problem with Vitzelly's system and similar variants of the martingale progression is that they require a rapid escalation in the value of the bets placed if the selected even-money chance does not come up. If pursued long enough, this escalation would consume the gambler's capital long before he could get into profit. A martingale progression starting with a £10 bet would require a bet of £20,480 after twelve successive losses, £163,840 after fifteen losses, and an astronomic £5,242,800 after twenty losses! Even if the gambler had a bankroll sufficiently large to finance the progression, no casino in the world would allow a bet of this size to be placed. The martingale bettor would consequently be eliminated before he could recoup his losses on a very bad run.

For this reason, the martingale betting system is doomed to ultimate failure, unless – as in the hypothetical situation posited by Professor Einstein – the gambler is able to play for all eternity with infinite capital.

Since Messrs Sala, Mayhew and Vitzelly did not have infinite capital, their fate was inevitable.

It need scarcely be said that our own expedition, in a financial sense, was a deplorable fiasco. We did not break the bank of Homburg, but the bank broke us; not swiftly, but with playful procrastination, such as is used by the cat when she plays with the mouse before devouring it. For about a week or two we adhered inflexibly to our infallible system and won about 700 pounds; then luck turned against us; we were unable to continue the doubling of our stakes, and in the course of one happy evening we lost 500 pounds.

Then, by common consent, we let the infallible system go hang; and each of us played according to his own fancy ... We had varied fortunes; on some nights we dreamed of thousands of pounds piled up in silken bags, of diamond bracelets, horses, dogs, and grounds, and alternate showerbaths of Heidseck's Dry Monopole and Jean Marie Farina's Eau de Cologne. On other days we borrowed gold coins from one another, and ultimately silver coins. In eleven days we were all stony broke. When our insolvency was complete, Vitzelly got a cheque for £25 cashed to pay our travelling expenses home.

Not many gamblers came away from Homburg richer, but some at least were a little wiser for the experience. Thirty years on, Sala reflected in his memoirs that 'at this present time of writing I look upon Vitzelly's system as perhaps the most idiotic of the innumerable imbecile systems evolved from distempered brains of gamblers'.

George Augustus Sala had learnt the truth about mathematical probability in roulette.

The Gambler's Fallacy

In 1903, Sir Hiram Maxim, distinguished engineer and inventor of the world's first automatic machine gun, wrote a letter to the Paris edition of the *New York Times*. In his letter, Sir Hiram argued that, because of the slight odds in favour of the bank in single-zero roulette, it was mathematically impossible to devise any staking system which could beat the game. He closed his letter by quoting the most famous casino proprietor of the previous century, François Blanc: 'The most sensible advice that may be given to would-be gamblers, or inventors of systems to be used at Monte Carlo, may be summed up in a single word – Don't!'

Maxim's apparently uncontroversial statements provoked a strong response from the aristocratic gamblers of Edwardian England. A long correspondence followed in the *New York Herald* and *The Times* of London, which included a letter from the Honourable Fitzroy S. Erskine. Writing to the *Herald* from Monte Carlo, the Honourable Fitzroy described his own system for beating the bank, and stated, 'I maintain that, with fair capital, good nerve, and an iron constitution, one can triumph over the much-vaunted *refait de la Maison*.' This letter was followed by one from Fitzroy's brother, Lord Rosslyn.

I quite agree with my brother that there is no flaw in his system. I might add that I would be willing to demonstrate the system in a private room to persons interested in it, who would make it worth my while to do so. I would demonstrate it to persons who would be willing to give it a trial at Monte Carlo. If a capital of £15,000 were employed, for instance, it would bring a return of £1,000 a day.

Lord Rosslyn's confidence in the efficacy of gambling systems had apparently not been dented by personal insolvency. For the noble Lord, far from being a successful gambler as might be inferred from the calm assurance of his epistle, was in fact merely one in a long line of ruined aristocrats who had lost their fortunes on the gaming tables.

Having inherited the title and a considerable estate in 1890, Lord Rosslyn had squandered over one hundred thousand pounds on the race tracks of England and the baize tables of Monte Carlo before being declared bankrupt in 1897. For some years thereafter, he eked out a humble existence as an actor and journalist.

The decline in his fortunes did not dampen his optimism. The particular system advocated by Lord Rosslyn and his brother in the columns of the *Herald* was to back an even-money chance such as red or black or odd or even. After staking one betting unit, he advocated that the gambler should then proceed to bet 3, 4, 5, 6, 7 and so on, until the gambler's win was equal to the number of spins of the wheel.

Whether he was aware of the fact or not, Lord Rosslyn's staking system closely resembled one used with some success in the eighteenth century by Jean le Rond d'Alembert. The crucial difference was that d'Alembert applied his system on a roulette wheel with no zero where the gambler's mathematically expected return was not -1.35 per cent, but 0 per cent. The rule laid down by d'Alembert was as follows: *a player should increase his bet by one unit after he loses, and decrease his bet by one unit after he wins.* Thus, a gambler backing an even-money chance on the roulette wheel starting with a £10 bet should increase it to £20, then £30, then £40, and so on as he loses; and reduce it as he wins, until he is back to the £10 starting bet.

This system has one major advantage compared to the martingale or doubling-up system. Since the betting progression is less steep, it requires less capital, and is less likely to hit the table limits before it starts to win. The system can be quite effective in fair games where the payoff on a winning bet is exactly equal to the mathematical expectation of that bet. D'Alembert was able to find such games in private houses during the eighteenth century. In these games, the role of the croupier was simply to redistribute bets between winners and losers, with no percentage taken by the house.

One example of the d'Alembert system will suffice to demonstrate how it works. In twenty spins of a fair roulette wheel on which there is no zero, let us assume that the red and black numbers each come up ten times. A player is backing the red numbers using the d'Alembert system, and the sequence shown in the table below occurs.

Spin no.	Win (loss)	Gambler's stake	Gambler's win (loss)	Cumulative win (loss)
1	(black)	£10	(£10)	(£10)
2	(black)	£20	(£20)	(£30)
3	red	£30	£30	£0
4	red	£20	£20	£20
5	(black)	£10	(£10)	£10
6	(black)	£20	(£20)	(£10)
7	red	£30	£30	£20
8	(black)	£20	(£20)	(£10)
9	(black)	£30	(£30)	(£40)
10	(black)	£40	(£40)	(£80)
11	(black)	£50	(£50)	(£130)
12	red	£60	£60	(£70)
13	red	£50	£50	(£20)
14	red	£40	£40	£20
15	(black)	£30	£30	(£10)
16	red	£40	£40	£30
17	red	£30	£30	£60
18	red	£20	£20	£80
19	(black)	£10	£10	£70
20	red	£20	£20	£90

With an equal number of red and black numbers, the system produces a comfortable profit for the d'Alembert bettor.

It may be objected that this result only arises because of the absence of a zero and the predominance of red numbers at the end of the sequence. It is the case that the d'Alembert bettor backing the black numbers would be down £50 after the twentieth spin (though breaking even after the nineteenth). However, if the d'Alembert bettor backs *both* the red and black simultaneously, varying the bet on each according to the d'Alembert principle, he or she would be £40 *ahead* in aggregate after the twentieth spin of the wheel. The profit of £90 from red would more than offset the £50 loss from black.

However, even in a fair game, the d'Alembert would generate losses if there were a long run of one colour or the other. In the example cited, the maximum loss is attained on the eleventh spin, after a run of four blacks. But if there were a freak run of, say, twenty red numbers in succession, the gambler would win £200 on twenty winning red bets of £10 each, but lose £2,100 on his escalating bets on the black, to realize a net loss of £1,900.

Although the chance of such a freak sequence is remote, it does illustrate a general principle. Even with a sound betting system, a gambler cannot expect to win all the time, and his or her bankroll must be adequate to cover occasional losing streaks. Consistent success at gambling is achieved, not through a few spectacular coups, but through a long, steady grind, where wins are punctuated by occasional steep losses. For this reason, a professional gambler would never place more than a small percentage of his bankroll on any bet. In particular, he would never use the martingale or doubling-up system, which, if taken to its limit, would imply that the gambler placed half his total bankroll on the final bet placed (prior to total ruination!).

In contrast, the d'Alembert has many of the characteristics of a sound betting system. It does not involve the gambler betting a disproportionate amount of his capital on any coup. This applies particularly if the gambler sets an upper limit on the maximum bet placed. For example, if the maximum bet is defined as twenty times the minimum bet, the gambler is protected against escalating losses should a freak run of more than twenty consecutive losses occur. Moreover, the d'Alembert is generally capable of generating winnings whichever way the gambler bets in a fair game or, better still, even if the gambler backs all possible outcomes.

Such would have been the reasoning behind Lord Rosslyn's advocacy of the system. However, in a game in which the gambler has a *negative* expectation such as single-zero roulette, the d'Alembert cannot generate consistent winnings for the gambler. Over the long haul it will result in losses just as surely as the martingale. The only consolation is that the losses will be less because of the slower progression of the d'Alembert. The gambler will lose the same percentage, but a lower total amount because a lower sum of money would be placed into action.

In his autobiography, Lord Rosslyn related how Sir Hiram Maxim took up his challenge.

In 1908 I met Sir Hiram Maxim, who challenged me to a match at my system, saying that there is no system to beat the odds at Monte Carlo. I accepted the challenge, as I knew that if I succeeded, I should get as much money as I wanted to go to Monte Carlo and try it.

We played in a room left us by Ralph Cobbold in Piccadilly, and I think we played six or seven hours a day ... The match was for £10 only, and if I retained my (theoretical) capital of £10,000 at the end of a fortnight, I was to be considered the winner.

At the end of the first week I had won £500, and there was considerable excitement, representatives of the press calling twice a day for information. But in the end I was left in a hopeless position, staking nearly £400 a spin with only about £1,200 left. One of the colours on the wheel predominated by nearly 60 per cent for a long period, and that was the cause of the defeat of one of the best systems ever invented.

My Gamble with Life

As reported in the London and Paris newspapers, the results of the last seven days of Lord Rosslyn's odyssey are shown in the table below.

Day	Spins	Cumulative win (loss)
8	350	(£547)
9	380	£1,648
10	380	£1,546
11	500	£274
12	500	£583
13	200	(£3,923)
14	380	(£10,340)

Twenty years later, the feckless Lord Rosslyn was still apparently convinced that he lost as a result of bad luck. The truth is that he lost because Sir Hiram Maxim was right: his system was fundamentally flawed and could not overcome the bank's edge. Even the d'Alembert betting progression could not withstand a long run of one colour or another, whose occurrence becomes more likely the longer play goes on.

Countless fortunes have been lost pursuing some betting progression built on a similarly flawed understanding of the law of averages. For example, there is an attested case of the roulette ball landing on an even number 27 times in succession on a wheel in Monte Carlo. Anyone betting that an odd number had to occur at some point according to the law of averages would have been cleaned out long before that run ended. Note that the probability of 27 successive occurrences of any event with a single-trial probability of $\frac{18}{37}$ is approximately 280 *million* to 1 against, being $\frac{18}{37}$ raised to its twenty-seventh power. These odds seem huge. Yet a mathematician would forecast such a result once in every 50 years in a casino with five roulette wheels, each spun approximately 500 times each day. Since the Grand Casino at Monte Carlo has now been open for well over 100 years, it would therefore be more surprising if some such run had *not* occurred during its history.

Bertrand Russell once observed that every time we see a car number plate we are witnessing a miracle, because the odds against any particular combination of letters and numbers are huge. Only when we happen to see a car number plate with our initials or birth date on it do we think anything unusual has occurred.

Most gambling systems are based upon betting against the occurrence of the improbable. They fail to take into account the fact that the improbable is one of a range of possible outcomes which in aggregate are certain. They also fail to acknowledge the fact that, as the number of trials within a Bernoulli process increases, it becomes more likely that an improbable event will occur at some point.

Perhaps the most endearing characteristic of gamblers is their eternal optimism. They are blessed with selective memories, enabling them to filter out the bad times and remember only the good. From Julius Caesar to Dostoevsky, gamblers through the ages have never complained or given up hope even when they have lost every penny. They are driven onwards by the gamblers' fallacy – that previous bad luck means there is a greater chance of future good fortune, because these matters even themselves up in the long run.

Popular betting systems have such a veneer of mathematical elegance that it is difficult to see the flaw that undermines them. One of the oldest systems is the Fibonnaci progression named after the thirteenth-century mathematician Leonardo Fibonnaci of Pisa whose *Liber Abaci* was the most influential medieval textbook on arithmetic. The most famous problem posed in the book was as follows: *how many pairs of rabbits will be produced each month, beginning with a single pair, if every month each 'productive' pair bears a new pair which becomes productive from the second month on?* The answer, month by month, is 1, 1, 2, 3, 5, 8, 13, 21 . . ., from which we can see that the number of pairs produced in any particular month is given by the sum of the pairs produced in each of the two preceding months.

The Fibonacci sequence was applied to other cases of biological growth. At some point, a medieval punter got hold of it and noted that if a gambler increased the bet on an even-money chance according to the sequence every time he lost, and decreased it by one after a win, he could generate a profit with just two successive wins irrespective of how great a loss had been suffered previously.

As a means of recovering a loss, it may be regarded as preferable to the martingale, because the escalation of the stake is less dramatic. Even so, a bad run will wipe out a Fibonacci bettor just as certainly as a martingale bettor.

Another popular system is the Labouchere betting progression. The Labouchere involves devising a series of numbers – any series, at the bettor's discretion – that adds up to the total win target. The first and last numbers in the series are added, and this becomes the initial bet. If the bet wins, the numbers are cancelled; and the bettor works inwards through the series until all the numbers have been cancelled, at which point the target win has been attained. On the other hand, if the bet loses, the value of the bet is added to the series, which has to be cancelled before the bettor progresses inwards.

The attraction of the system is that, while only one number is added to the series if a bet *loses*, two numbers are cancelled after a *win*. Thus the Labouchere progression apparently offers a 2-1 proposition on an even-money bet.

The weakness of the system is that the bet size steadily escalates after a series of losses. The rate of escalation is not as rapid as with the martingale but is equally certain to hit the table's upper bet limit or wipe out the gambler's bankroll in a long enough series of trials.

The martingale, Fibonacci and Labouchere betting progressions all share the same weakness. They offer the prospect of escalating losses for a strictly limited gain. In the case of the martingale, the gain is the initial bet unit placed; in the case of the Fibonacci, the net gain after two successive wins is just one bet unit; and in the case of the Labouchere, the total possible gain is the value of the initial series. All three systems envisage the gambler eventually bludgeoning his way to success by committing sums of money which may be far greater than the prospective gain in order to pursue the system to its bitter end. Most of the time this crude approach will be successful; but on the occasions it is not, the catastrophic losses suffered by the gambler will not only wipe out all previous profits, but also give the house its percentage on top.

If a gambler has to use a betting system, a less dangerous proposition would be one that limits the possible losses while setting no limit to possible gains. One such system is the reverse Labouchere, whereby the amount of each win is added to the bet series, while the two outside numbers are cancelled after each loss. Most of the time the gambler will post a small loss. On the other hand, the gains from a series of wins could be spectacular. In fact, the probable pattern is the mirror image of the Labouchere – most sessions will end with a small loss, but in a few sessions the gambler will enjoy a spectacular win. Mathematically, the expectation is exactly the same over a long series of trials. The gambler will lose a percentage of the money he gambles equal to the house's edge. The pattern of this loss changes, but not the final percentage.

The only advice that can be given to those rash enough to try their luck in a negative expectation game such as roulette or dice is as follows: set aside a limited amount of capital you are prepared to lose; bet aggressively within the limitations of this capital; and leave immediately you have lost it or played for an hour or so. Do not play longer, for the longer you play, the more likely it becomes that you will be ruined.

Better still, give up roulette.

If you must go on gambling, consider taking up a positive expectation game – that is, a game where the gambler can, under certain conditions, gain an edge over the bank.

A game such as blackjack.

BLACKJACK

The Legend of the Little Dark-haired Guy from California

Sometime during the 1950s, a mysterious individual who has gone down in the annals of gambling folklore simply as 'the little dark-haired guy from California' approached certain Nevada casinos with an interesting proposition. He offered to take them on in a no-limits blackjack game. There would be no restrictions on the amount the player could bet, and the game would continue until either the player or the casino decided to quit.

Without too much hesitation, the casinos accepted the challenge. They were confident that they enjoyed an edge over the player, since they knew that their profit from the game over the years had amounted to between 3 and 5 per cent of the total amount bet. The size of the house edge could not be defined as precisely as in roulette or dice games because it depended not only on the mathematics of the game but also on the playing decisions exercised by the gambler. Nevertheless, the casinos were certain that over a long series of plays their edge would be decisive.

Play continued over several evenings. Whatever casino the little Californian played in, the story was always the same. For the first few evenings, the advantage fluctuated between the player and the house – sometimes the player was ahead, sometimes the casino; but neither side gained an overwhelming advantage. The pattern resembled the first ten days of the contest between Sir Hiram Maxim and Lord Rosslyn half a century earlier. There were other similarities. The mystery player seemed to be using a progressive betting system, just as Lord Rosslyn had. The game was dealt from a single deck of cards and as it was depleted through successive rounds of play the gambler would frequently increase the size of his bet, before reverting to his original stake after the cards were shuffled.

The casinos may not have been aware of the precise details of Lord Rossyln's experiment, but they had observed a lot of similar attempts to overcome the house edge by means of a progressive betting system. They knew that a gambler with a large bankroll, applying a system such as the d'Alembert where the progression was modest rather than violent, had a reasonable chance of coming out ahead in the short term. Consequently they were not perturbed by the fact that it seemed to be taking some time to grind down the player from California. They accepted that the results would fluctuate from one evening to another, in line with the predictions of de Moivre's theorem. But they also knew that the longer play continued, the more likely it would be that these fluctuations would cancel each other out in the house's favour. The final result would be that the casino would win the challenger's bankroll.

They were wrong. By a process of observation and analysis, the little dark-haired guy was gaining an edge over the casino. Three or four nights into the challenge, he had got the casino to accept wide swings in the size of his bet and the total value of the wins and losses of each side.

The casino was now primed for the kill. It was about to receive an expensive education in the mathematics of blackjack.

The game of blackjack, also known as twenty-one, Van John and pon-toon, had arrived in Nevada by way of the trenches of First World War Flanders, where the allied troops had played the game to while away the hours of waiting before battle. The same characteristics that attrac-ted the troops to it made it ideal for casino gambling.

First, blackjack is a straight adversarial confrontation between the dealer and the players. Second, the number of participants is flexible – anywhere between one and a dozen players can challenge the dealer in a game of blackjack. Third, the game can be set up easily, and can be abandoned after any hand without interrupting the flow of play – an essential feature for soldiers who might be called to arms at any moment. Each hand was resolved in a matter of a minute or two, after which the dealer could pay any winners, collect losing bets, and put the cards in his kitbag. Blackjack thus differs from card games such as bridge and whist where the final result depends on a series of hands.

A further characteristic of blackjack which made it suitable for both the trenches and the casinos was the simplicity of its rules. While an individual requires some training to master bidding and playing techniques in bridge, anyone can pick up blackjack after a few minutes spent watching others play.

The precise rules of the game vary from country to country. In Las Vegas and Atlantic City, they vary from casino to casino. In London and the rest of the UK, the rules are standard and are dictated by the British Gaming Board. Whatever the precise rules of the game, the principles of play are the same the world over.

The object of the game is for the player to beat the dealer by drawing cards with a combined total that will exceed the value of the dealer's hand, but not exceed 21. If a player draws a card that takes the total to above 21, that hand is bust and the player loses his stake.

The value of court cards (jacks, queens and kings) is 10. Aces are valued as either 1 or 11, at the player's discretion. All other cards between 2 and 10 have their face value. Thus, a hand of 9 and 6 would have a value of 15; a hand of 4, 5 and jack would have a value of 19; and a hand of 8 and king would have a value of 18. A hand comprising an ace and a 9 could in principle be valued as either 10 (1+9) or 20 (11+9); in practice, a player playing under British rules would always value the hand as 20, and elect to stand rather than draw further cards.

The procedures in British casinos are as follows. Four decks of cards are shuffled by the dealer in front of the players. The dealer then invites one of the players to cut the cards, inserts a joker or cut card 40–70 cards from the bottom of the pack, and places the cards in a dealing box or shoe from which the dealer draws the cards. All cards are dealt face-up, and at no time are any of the players permitted to touch any of the cards.

Each player plays independently against the dealer. The dealer deals two cards to each player, and one card to himself. If there is only a single player at the table, that player must play at least two hands.

The players draw first in the sequence in which the cards were dealt. They each decide whether they wish to draw more cards or stand with their existing hand. They indicate their decision to the dealer either verbally (by saying 'card' or 'draw' if they wish to draw, and 'stand' to indicate they have completed their hand) or by physical gesture. The standard gestures are as follows: in order to draw another card, a player taps the table in front of him; in order to stand, the player passes his hand downwards from right to left over the cards. At no time is the player permitted to touch the cards themselves.

In addition to the option of drawing further cards, the players have two other options.

The first is that if the first two cards dealt are of equal value (such as two 7s or two 8s), the player can split them. If a player wishes to split, he places a second bet of equal value to the first bet alongside it. The dealer then separates the two cards and the player plays them as two separate hands. Under British rules, players are not permitted to re-split: for example, if a player is dealt two 8s and splits them, and is then dealt another 8 on one of the hands, he must play that hand as 16 and elect to draw or stand on it. Players may draw as many additional cards to split hands as they like, with the exception of split aces. Players are only permitted to draw one additional card to each split ace. Under British rules, players may not split 4s, 5s or 10s (including court cards).

The second option available to the player is to double the bet. If a player wishes to double, he places a second bet of equal value to the first bet in the betting box, and is then permitted to draw one extra card only. Under British rules, players may only double their bet on two-card totals of 9, 10 or 11 which do not include an ace (for example, a two-card hand of 6–3 or 7–4).

If a player draws to a two-card total of 9, 10 or 11 after splitting the cards (for example, drawing a 2 or a 3 to the split 8), then he or she is allowed to double the bet and then receive one additional card only on that hand. Consequently, it is possible that a player could multiply an original bet fourfold if dealt a hand that contained two cards of equal value which were split and then drew to two-card totals of 9, 10 or 11 on each of them, which he elected to double.

The final outcome of the hand depends partly on the cards dealt to the player, and partly on the skill with which the player exercises the options available. There is a mathematically optimal strategy for play against a randomly shuffled shoe of cards which is described in detail in Appendix II (p.154).

While the player has a number of options in choosing how to play, the dealer must play according to a predetermined set of rules. The dealer cannot split or double, and must draw on totals less than 17 and stand on totals of between 17 and 21. A dealer hand of ace–6 is valued as 17 (not 7) and the dealer must stand on this hand. If the dealer draws to a total greater than 21, he is bust and must pay all the bets of players remaining in the game.

If neither player nor dealer bust, the winner is the adversary with a final total closer to 21. If they both hold cards of equal combined value, the hand is a tie and no money changes hands. Thus, if a player has a final hand with a total of 18, he wins if the dealer draws to 17 or busts; he loses if the dealer draws to 19, 20 or 21; and he ties if the dealer also draws to 18. All bets are paid off at even-money odds of 1–1: that is, 1 unit paid for each unit bet.

The only exception to the even-money pay-off occurs if a player draws a two-card total of 21, comprising an ace and 10 or court card. This hand of ace–10 is a 'natural' 21, or blackjack, and is paid at the bonus rate of 3–2: that is, the player is paid 3 units for every 2 units bet.

If a player is dealt a natural two-card 21 and the dealer shows an ace as his first card, the player may opt to take 'insurance' and be paid at even money (1 unit for each unit bet) before the dealer draws a second card. If the player does not take insurance and the dealer then draws a 10, the player and dealer tie and no money changes hands.

The dealer's advantage in drawing last is critical. If any of the players busts, the dealer always wins their bets – even if the dealer then goes on to bust. It is this fact that tilts the odds in the dealer's favour. Because the dealer draws last, no matter how skilfully the player exercises the options available, the dealer will win more hands than the player over a long series of plays.

Since the dealer is mathematically certain to win the majority of hands played, it would appear impossible for the player to win more bets than he loses.

Or so, at least, it was believed in the Nevada casinos of the 1950s, when the mysterious Californian gambler arrived with his proposition. The casinos were confident that, although the player might win in the short term, over the long term any positive fluctuation would be ironed out and the gambler would be ground down into losses.

But even in the 1950s, there were a few gamblers who had realized a critical fact about the game of blackjack. Although the dealer was guaranteed to win the majority of *hands* played, it did not mean that he would win most of the *money* wagered. If the player bet more money on the few hands he won than on the majority of hands he lost, he could come out ahead in the long run.

Of course, this is no different from the pipe-dream of thousands of roulette system players through the ages. But while the betting progressions employed by system players were founded on fallacies regarding the law of averages, the most expert blackjack players were able to use legitimate mathematical means to predict when the cards were in their favour. Very few individuals knew how the player could gain an edge over the dealer in blackjack. The secret was passed from one gambler to another by word of mouth and it was only revealed to those who could be trusted not to reveal it to the casinos. The Californian gambler was one of the initiates of this secret society.

According to the American casino executive Mike Goodman, systems to beat casino blackjack date back at least to the 1930s. In *Your Best Bet*, Goodman relates how he was taught how to count cards in 1939 by 'an old card hustler called Shimkey' who 'never worked a day in his life' but 'travelled back and forth across the country looking for 21 games'.

Shimkey was barred from play by casinos throughout the USA.

The casinos and dealers began wondering why Shimkey always won. They couldn't catch him doing anything, but they figured he must be doing something, so, one by one, the clubs barred Shimkey from the tables. That's why he came to me. I was also hustling cards in those days, and our paths crossed several times. He wanted to teach me his count method, and then we would split the winnings.

Your Best Bet

By his own account, Goodman won $1,250 in a week using the system.

It was the easiest money I had ever made. At $1,250 a week, it wouldn't be long before I would have my own casino. A nice dream, but the next night, which was my eighth night in the club, the top boss came over to a 21 table as I sat down and asked me into his office.
'Mike, my boy,' he said, 'you're a nice lad, but you're a little too lucky in here. We can't nail you doing anything to the cards, but I think you'd better play somewhere else from now on.'

Your Best Bet

Goodman then claimed that he was really an unemployed dealer, whereupon the pit boss offered him a job which, in the circumstances, he could hardly refuse. And so Goodman began working on the other side of the tables. In his job as a casino executive, he had no compunction in taking counter-measures against other card players.

Shimkey and Goodman are unusual in having been barred from play. It appears that very few players were barred from playing the game before the publication of Dr Thorp's *Beat the Dealer*. Those players who could beat the game were generally allowed to play unmolested, either because they were sufficiently canny to conceal their skill, or because the casinos simply did not regard them as a significant threat.

One of the most remarkable early players was Benjamin F. Smith, known as 'System Smitty', who spent several years playing out 100,000 hands in order to determine an accurate playing system for the game. However, System Smitty did not calculate a detailed strategy for doubling down or splitting. As a result of the weaknesses in his system, he won irregularly and experienced violent fluctuations in his playing capital. On one occasion, he was reported to have won $108,000 at the blackjack tables during the course of an evening's play, only to lose it all by the following morning.

One of the players to whom System Smitty passed his secrets was a certain Mr X, a wealthy gambler who was later to team up with Dr Edward Thorp.

According to a 1984 article by Dr Thorp in the *Gambling Times Guide to Blackjack*,

Smitty's system, which was first used in the mid-1950s, seems to have spread to a small group of players including an old-time gambler whom we shall call the Silver Fox, the Fox's mistress, Mr X, the 'little dark-haired guy from California', and a young player commonly known as both 'Junior' and 'Sonny'.

This group of players pumped large sums of money out of the blackjack tables within the next few years. There is no way to determine exactly how large these sums were. For what it is worth, the grapevine credits the Silver Fox with $50,000 of winnings and Mr X with $100,000 to $150,000 gross. The little dark-haired guy is supposed to have cleared $250,000.

According to Jon Bradshaw's book *Fast Company*, the true identity of the Silver Fox was none other than Jay Bernstein, who was one of the participants in a notorious card game in New York which continued for more than 30 hours between 8 and 10 September 1928 and led to the slaying of Arnold Rothstein. Rothstein was shot on 4 November 1928 and died two days later without revealing the name of his assailant. He died owing Jay Bernstein $69,000 and the other participants in the game a total of $404,000.

When questioned about Rothstein's death, the Silver Fox stated, not unreasonably, that even if he had had the opportunity to kill him, he would have had no motive to do so, since he could not collect his $69,000 gambling debt from a dead man.

No one was ever charged with Rothstein's killing. However, according to Jon Bradshaw, the game's participants were aware that he was shot accidentally by the game's organizer George McManus during a dispute over the settlement of his gambling debts. Ironically the day Rothstein died was the same day as the American presidential election on which he had placed a large winning bet. Had he lived, he would have collected over a half a million dollars and been able to pay off all his debts.

The circumstances of Rothstein's death – the fact that he himself did not reveal the name of the man who shot him, and the wall of silence which subsequently descended over the incident – illustrates the unwritten code of loyalty binding together the tiny band of high-rolling gamblers. They are also an extreme manifestation of the problem of the gamblers' ruin, whereby a gambler can lose all his money even when playing with a long-run positive expectation if he overbets his limited capital and leaves himself vulnerable to a short-run negative fluctuation.

Despite the fact that he never collected the $69,000 that Arnold Rothstein owed him, the Silver Fox made a comfortable if volatile living from gambling over the next forty years. The Fox gambled on racing and sports as well as card games, and was probably among the dozen or so most successful blackjack players of the 1940s and 1950s.

His winnings pale in comparison to those of the Californian gambler. According to *Beat the Dealer*, Dr Thorp was informed by one casino in the early 1960s that it had been challenged by many system players, but had only found it necessary to bar one. This was a player whom the casino identified simply as 'the little dark-haired guy from California'.

The casino related how the Californian had acted as a wealthy high roller from whom they should have been able to win substantial sums. He built up this image by asking for a private game for a minimum stake of $25 a hand in a single-deck game dealt down to the last card. During the course of the game he would first win large amounts and then lose slightly larger amounts over a series of evenings.

When it appeared that the casino was used to these wide swings, and was primed to believe that it was only a matter of time before the gambler's luck would run out, he went for the kill, playing to win for tens of thousands of dollars. The casino had absorbed losses of more than $50,000 before it eventually realized that it had been stung, and called off the game.

The casino had no idea of how the Californian had done it, but by the time it called a halt it knew that he definitely had the edge over the dealer, and that prolonging the game would merely increase the casino's losses. For one of the few times in the history of casino gambling, the casino had been frozen out by a gambler.

The gambler repeated his coup in a number of Nevada casinos. He was aided by the fact that few people witnessed the private games in which he played, and those who did had no desire to advertise the fact that they had lost heavily. It was some time before the sting became so widely known that he was unable to use it. By the time he had been barred from every casino in Nevada, it is estimated that he had won over quarter of a million dollars. In today's money, eroded by more than thirty years of inflation, that win would be equivalent to well over a million dollars.

In essence, his sting was similar to a pool-room hustle where the hustler appears like a barely competent loser who experiences just enough luck to encourage him to go on playing for ever larger stakes. Only when the hustler's victim is well primed, and has more money on the game than he ever intended to bet initially, does the hustler reveal his true colours and play to his full ability.

There is a certain poetic justice about the losses suffered by the casinos. They fell victim to his proposition through a mixture of greed (knowing that he had a substantial bankroll) and arrogance (believing that they had fixed the odds so that they could not possibly be beaten). The little dark-haired guy then turned their greed and arrogance against them to relieve them of a large slice of the money they had lifted from mug punters.

The casinos had no idea of how the gambler had won his fortune, but it would not be long before they found out. The truth was about to be revealed by one of the most original minds ever applied to gambling problems.

The Gambling Mathematician

At this point, one of the heroes of this book re-enters the story. This is the young Dr Edward O. Thorp of the University College of Los Angeles (UCLA).

Dr Thorp followed in a long tradition of mathematicians who have applied scientific methods to gain an edge in games of chance, and who have gone on to prove their ideas by applying them successfully to win modest fortunes.

The history of gambling is pockmarked by such anti-heroes, often social outcasts who could only make their way in the world by living off their wits in games of chance. In the sixteenth century, Gerolamo Cardano survived an attempt by his mother to abort him before birth to publish the first solutions on cubic and quartic equations in *Artis magnae sive de regulis algebraicis* (*The Art of Solving Algebraic Equations*, Nuremberg, 1545). On a less elevated level, Cardano also wrote *Liber de Ludo Aleae* (*The Book on Games of Chance*, published posthumously in 1663), in which he applied the concept of mathematical expectation to the solution of gambling problems. In the seventeenth century Abraham de Moivre, a refugee from religious persecution in France, eked out a living on the card tables of London; his central limit theorem remains one of the cornerstones of statistics. In the eighteenth century, Jean le Rond d'Alembert, who took his name from the Church of St Jean le Rond in Paris where he had been abandoned at birth by his mother, survived to become a successful gambler and respected mathematician, and was the mentor of perhaps the greatest of all exponents of probability theory, the Marquis de Laplace.

Into this tradition of gambling mathematicians stepped Dr Thorp at the end of the 1950s. He was not the first person to comprehend that the game of blackjack could be beaten by mathematical methods, but he was the first person to apply a highly trained scientific mind to the analysis of the game and to publish his results for wider dissemination.

Although blackjack in its various forms has a history going back several centuries, it was not until the 1950s that a group of scientists first tried to calculate the mathematically optimal strategy for the game. The group comprised Roger Baldwin, Wilbert Cantey, Herbert Maisel and James McDermott, who together worked out the probabilities for each possible playing option on desk calculators while they were stationed at the US Army Base in Aberdeen, Maryland, between 1953 and 1956. Their results were published in the *Journal of the American Statistical Association* under the title 'The Optimum Strategy in Blackjack' in 1956.

This pioneering effort did not gain a lot of attention. It was initially regarded as an academic exercise of little interest to professional gamblers. The reason appears to have been that the Baldwin group established that the mathematically optimal method of playing blackjack was a losing strategy. In other words, they calculated that even if a player played according to this method he or she would lose in the long run. The optimal strategy would merely lose at a slower rate than any alternative strategy. This conclusion did not appear to offer much hope for the professional gambler.

However, one individual did take notice of the Baldwin paper. The young Dr Edward Thorp was at that time an impoverished postgraduate student of physics who was seeking to 'shatter the chains of poverty through a scientifically-based winning gambling system'. His interest in the game was stimulated when he used the Baldwin basic strategy in a Nevada casino and discovered, much to his surprise, that it seemed to work. He lost money playing the game, but he lost at a slower rate than other players, and often won hands that he expected to lose by making plays which seemed intuitively poor, but were in fact mathematically correct.

Thorp's fascination with the game led him to reflect upon it further. He realized that the basic strategy derived by the Baldwin group depends upon two pieces of information. The first is the value of the cards in the player's hand, and the second is the value of the dealer's up card.

There is one further assumption: that the cards remaining to be dealt from the shoe are randomly distributed and are in proportion to a standard deck of 52 cards. Thus, the chance of drawing a card with a value of 10 (that is, a 10, jack, queen or king) is assumed to be 30.77 per cent, or 16/52, since there are 16 cards with a value of 10 in a standard deck of 52 cards. Acting upon this assumption, the player who holds two cards with a value of 11 (say 5 plus 6) can confidently double down against a dealer's 5 in the knowledge that there is a good chance of drawing to 18, 19, 20 or 21, and that if he fails to do so there is a good chance that the dealer will draw high cards and bust. Either way, the player stands to win. The precise probabilities in fact indicate that the player dealt a total of 11 against a dealer's 5 can expect to win two-thirds of the hands and lose one-third (ignoring ties). Thus, the player enjoys a 2–1 positive expectation on this hand, which should almost always be exploited by doubling the initial bet.

However, the assumption that the cards still to be dealt mirror the structure of a standard deck of cards may be wildly inaccurate. For example, if a large number of 10s and court cards have already been dealt, there would only be a few cards with a value of 10 remaining to be dealt. Therefore there would be considerably less chance of drawing a 10-value card than the 30.77 per cent assumed by basic strategy. In this case, the basic strategy player who confidently doubles the bet on 11 against a dealer's 5 may have a nasty surprise in store if he is then dealt a low card and the dealer also draws low cards to end with a pat hand of between 17 and 21.

Contemplating such situations, Edward Thorp had the flash of brilliance that was to revolutionize the game of blackjack. He realized that *blackjack is not a Bernoulli system*. It is not a series of independent trials in which the probability of any outcome remains constant. In this crucial respect, it is unlike other casino games such as roulette and dice. In blackjack, the chances of being dealt any particular card fluctuates from one deal to the next depending on what cards have already been dealt. For example, there is a chance of $\frac{4}{52}$ or $\frac{1}{13}$ of being dealt an ace from a randomly shuffled deck of cards, since four of the 52 cards in the deck are aces. However, if the first four cards dealt from a new deck are aces, then the probability of being dealt an ace as the fifth card falls to zero.

Consequently, another property of Bernoulli systems does not hold. The outcome of different hands in blackjack are not independent of one another. The result of each deal affects the results of later deals from the same deck or shoe of cards. Therefore the probabilities of a player or dealer win vary from one hand to the next.

In December 1960, one month before John F. Kennedy took the oath of office as President of the United States, Thorp published a synopsis of his ideas under the title of 'Fortune's Formula: The Game of Blackjack' in *Notices of the American Mathematical Society*. His synopsis gained extensive newspaper coverage in journals such as the *Boston Globe, Las Vegas Sun* and *Washington Post*, and he was approached by a number of gamblers interested in providing financial backing to test his ideas in the Nevada casinos.

From the range of offers he received, Thorp selected two from millionaire gamblers whom he identifies simply as Mr X and Mr Y. Mr X was one of the small number of gamblers already capable of beating the game with crude card-counting methods which he had learnt from System Smitty.

The three partners devised a card-counting system based on tracking the number of 10-valued cards relative to non-10s dealt, and calculating the ratio remaining in the deck. In a standard 52-card deck, there are 16 cards with a value of 10 in blackjack: four 10s, four jacks, four queens and four kings. The remaining 36 cards have a value other than 10. Thus the ratio of non-10s to 10s is $\frac{36}{16}$, or 2.25. As the cards are dealt out, the ratio fluctuates according to the proportion of 10s and non-10s seen.

Dr Thorp observed that the player's advantage was related to the proportion of 10-valued cards among the cards still to be dealt, for three main reasons.

First, the player can choose to stand on totals between 12 and 16, while the dealer must draw – and the chances of the dealer busting go up if there are a lot of 10-value cards to be dealt.

Second, the player is paid 3–2 on natural two-card totals of 21 (blackjacks), while the dealer wins even money only by collecting the player's bet. With any given number of aces, the probability of dealing a blackjack rises with the number of 10-value cards, and this is to the player's advantage.

Third, the player's options for doubling and splitting become more valuable as the proportion of 10s increases. If the player doubles on a total of 9, 10 and 11, he or she may only draw one extra card and would prefer it to be a 10 to reach a total of 19, 20 or 21, which normally constitute winning hands. If the player splits aces, he or she is allowed only one more card and would like to draw a 10 to reach a total of 21. Other splitting options also become more valuable if there is a high proportion of 10s still to be dealt.

Dr Thorp noted that, while a predominance of high cards favours the player, a predominance of low cards favours the dealer. The reasons are the converse of those cited above: a high proportion of low cards makes it less likely that the dealer will bust, or that blackjacks will be dealt, or that doubled totals of 9, 10 or 11 will draw to winning totals; and implies that the player's option of splitting any two cards of equal value will be less rewarding.

However, if the player *knows* that the deck is rich in small cards, he can adjust the playing strategy to reflect this knowledge. The player can place a low bet so that he doesn't risk too much initially; he can refrain from doubling down on 9 or 10; and he can draw on 12, 13 or 14 knowing that there is a good chance of drawing a card with a value of 7 or less, so that his hand will be improved rather than busted.

If a player knows what cards to expect, he can minimize the dealer's advantage. At all times he is playing according to probabilities, not certainties; but while individual hands may go wrong, over a long series of hands an accurate assessment of the probability of drawing certain cards can swing the game in the player's favour if he plays and bets skilfully.

Dr Thorp's method of assessing probabilities involved tracking the ratio of non-10s to 10s waiting to be dealt. At the start of the deal, that ratio was 2.25. As the cards were dealt out, the ratio would fluctuate. If it fell – indicating a higher proportion of 10s and court cards among the undealt cards – the player's advantage would rise. Dr Thorp's team planned to exploit this by betting larger amounts in proportion to their estimated advantage. Their betting strategy involved

betting twice the amount of the minimum bet when the advantage is 1 per cent, four times the minimum when the advantage is 2 per cent, and finally levelling off at ten times the minimum when the advantage is 5 per cent or more in the player's favour. I determined that if my bets would range from $50 to $500 (the highest casino maximum generally available), then $6,000 or $7,000 would probably be adequate capital. To be safe, we took along $10,000 – a hundred one-hundred-dollar bills.

Beat the Dealer

In a single-deck game, I estimate that Dr Thorp's team could have expected to win approximately 2 per cent of all bets placed applying these rules. Note that such a win percentage would be impossible to achieve consistently in contemporary British casinos. The principal reason for this is that the contemporary British game is dealt out of a four-deck shoe, whereas the Thorp team played against a single deck of cards, often dealt out right to the last card. This implies that the Thorp team would have played against favourable decks far more frequently than any contemporary player would because, as Professor Peter Griffin observes in *The Theory of Blackjack*,

the important thing to realize is how many cards must be removed from multiple decks before they become as interesting as a single deck. Seeing one card from a single deck entitles us to as much excitement as will glimpsing 33 cards from six decks.

It was, of course, precisely these considerations that led the casinos to increase the number of decks with which the game was played after the publication of *Beat the Dealer* in 1962, in which Dr Thorp explained his ideas and described how he had applied them in practice.

Arriving in Nevada during UCLA's spring recess of 1961, Dr Thorp prudently tested his system at lower bet levels before advancing to the fifty-dollar tables. The training session was successful, although during the course of it Dr Thorp abandoned his mechanical betting rules as he noted that the sudden change of bet size attracted too much casino attention. Instead, he adopted the tactic of letting his bet ride in favourable situations – that is, letting a 1 unit bet ride to 2 units if it won, and then to 4 units if it won again. Dr Thorp observed that

this pattern of play resembles the well-known doubling up system, or small martingale, which is widely used in almost every gambling game ... Since the system is so widely and so unsuccessfully practised, it makes an excellent disguise for the counting player.

Beat the Dealer

With the act thus tested and refined, the team proceeded to the $500-maximum tables. At Harold's Club in Reno they won a modest amount before the casino started to apply counter-measures by shuffling the cards after only two hands had been played. At the next casino they visited, they were losing when Thorp was dealt a pair of 8s against the dealer's 6 with a bet of $300 on the table. He split the 8s and was dealt a 3 on one of them for a total of 11, which he doubled. There was now $900 on the table. The dealer drew two high cards to his 6 and busted.

With this win of $900 on a single hand, the team's fortunes began to improve. Dr Thorp noted that 'the system had shown a feature that would appear repeatedly: moderately heavy losing streaks, mixed with "lucky streaks" of the most dazzling brilliance'.

The team now began to win steadily; but by this time the Nevada casinos were beginning to get wind of their activities. They were barred from play in a Reno casino. They moved on to Lake Tahoe, where they had a spectacular win of $17,000 in two hours at Harvey's Wagon Wheel. Ed Thorp, tired from the effort of counting the cards for two hours, decided to cash in. At this point, human frailty jeopardized the scientific method of their enterprise.

After wending my way back to the tables, I watched, horror-stricken. Mr X, having refused to stop playing, was pouring back thousands. In the forty-five minutes that it took to persuade him to leave, it cost the two of us about $11,000 of our $17,000.

They were still ahead for the trip, but then proceeded to lose a further $2,000 on a series of visits to a casino with poor rules and five to ten cards cut out of play. This was regarded as a high number of cards to cut out in those halcyon days of the single-deck game – today, no casino in the world would shuffle the cards with only five cards remaining. In Britain, casinos typically cut at least 40 cards out of play from a four-deck shoe.

Dr Thorp, Mr X and Mr Y moved on to another club where they began winning, whereupon the pit boss carefully checked the backs of the cards for marking. He discovered none. Nevertheless, the house brought in four new decks in five minutes to pre-empt the possibility that Thorp was predicting which cards were about to be dealt by distinguishing tiny blemishes on their backs.

After disposing of that particular house theory, I pressed them to tell us what they thought was my 'secret'. The dealer claimed then that I could count every card as it was played, and that therefore I knew exactly which cards had not been played at each and every instant . . . I challenged the dealer by rashly claiming that no one in the world could watch 35 cards dealt quickly off a pack and then tell me quickly how many of each card remained.

She answered by claiming that the pit boss next to her could do just that. I told them I would pay $5 on the spot for a demonstration. They both looked down sheepishly and would not answer. I made my offer $50. They remained silent and ashamed. Then my friend Mr Y increased the offer to $500. There was no response from these 'sportsmen'. We left in disgust.

The moral was clear. Even though they did not know how it was done, the casinos would bar any players who won consistently.

It was the end of Dr Thorp's experiment. His team's bankroll had more than doubled, with the initial bank of $10,000 increased by a profit of $11,000 to a total of $21,000. They would have earned a further $11,000 had it not been for Mr X's disastrous foray.

The main consequences of Thorp's successful experiment were threefold. It proved once and for all that the player could gain an edge in blackjack by mathematical means. Unfortunately, Thorp's book also let the casinos in on the secret of how it could be done, and indicated how they could neutralize the player's potential edge.

This led to the second main consequence of the book. The casinos changed the rules and the conditions under which the game was played, to make it much more difficult – and in some cases impossible – for even the most skilful player to gain an edge. In particular, the number of decks used for the game was increased. One-deck games became increasingly rare; they were supplanted by four-deck, six-deck, or even eight-deck games, dealt out of shoes rather than by hand. The cut card was inserted some way from the end of the shoe, to prevent 'end-play' of the type described in *Beat the Dealer*, which had been one of the techniques used by the little dark-haired guy from California to relieve the Nevada casinos of quarter of a million dollars.

The book also gave the casinos invaluable tips on what to look for in card-counting players. The main symptom was a wide bet spread. Any player with a large bet on the table when high cards were dealt would henceforth be suspect. Such was the concern of casinos about the possibility of being beaten by skilful players that they barred an increasing number of gamblers from the game.

Thus emerged the third main consequence of *Beat the Dealer*. Players could win, but they would be permitted to go on winning only if the casino management was convinced that they were losing. Mastering the mathematics of the game was only the first condition of success at the blackjack tables. A more important condition from now on would be that the player should dissimulate his or her skill.

Masters of Disguise

The methods used by gamblers to gain an edge in the games in which they participate reflect the times in which they live. The attempts of our Victorian forebears to beat the roulette wheel were based on classical probability theory. The development of systems to beat the game of blackjack over the last thirty years would not have been possible without high-speed electronic computers. System Smitty tried and failed to devise an accurate playing strategy by dealing out hundreds of thousands of hands of cards to himself. The Baldwin Group were more successful in approximating a basic strategy for the game with the aid of manual calculators, but even this took many years of work. The advanced analysis of the game undertaken by Dr Thorp and the mathematicians who followed him was only possible with the assistance of computer technology to simulate the effects of the removal of different cards on player advantage.

Dr Thorp's system, in common with all winning systems developed since, relies on the player being able to predict what cards are likely to be dealt.

It is sometimes said that skilful bridge players are able to 'see' the cards. By making deductions about the distribution of the cards from the way other players bid and play, they can visualize where each card is held. This information enables them to win the critical marginal tricks on which the outcome of a playing session depends.

Masters of blackjack can also 'see' the cards still in the shoe. Using information gleaned from the cards already dealt they are able to assess the likelihood of high or low cards being dealt. The way in which they are able to do this is by *counting* the cards as they are dealt. The purpose of a card count is to give the player a mental picture of the composition of the cards still to be dealt. This mental picture is then used to help make decisions about how to bet and play.

Following the publication of *Beat the Dealer*, a bizarre assortment of mathematicians and gamblers embarked on a quest for the perfect card count. Dr Thorp led the quest with his ultimate point count, whose name suggested that it was the optimum to which a counter could aspire. Some of those who followed, such as Harvey Dubner with his hi-lo count and Charles Einstein with what became hi-opt I, sought perfect simplicity – the count that would yield the highest returns for the least effort. Others desired the greatest possible efficiency for betting and playing, and devised highly complex counts which often entailed keeping separate counts of aces.

A summary of some of the principal card-counting systems is included in Appendix II. The Appendix also contains an exposition of the main or zen count system, which is one of the most efficient single-parameter counting systems, and playing-strategy indices for its use in casino play.

Among the most prolific producers of blackjack card-counting systems was a professional gambler who operated under a number of aliases, of which the best known was Lawrence Revere. It was Revere's dream to devise a perfect system. He failed, for the truth is that there is no perfect card-counting system for casino blackjack. There are a multitude of counting systems which could be used to gain a slight edge over the casino if accurately applied, but none is 100 per cent accurate for betting and playing purposes.

The principal reason for this relates to the ambiguous nature of the ace. For betting purposes, the ace is a high card which helps the player. However, for playing purposes the ace is a low card that will never bust the player. Consequently systems which assign a count value to the ace have a high betting efficiency but a relatively low playing efficiency; while the reverse is true for systems which do not assign a value to the ace.

This problem could be partially overcome by keeping a separate count of the number of aces dealt, as Lawrence Revere did in his advanced point counts. However, one of the most important findings of the mathematical analysis of card counting is that, as in other fields of human endeavour, the law of diminishing returns applies. A computer could track every card separately and compute precise probabilities for each card instantaneously. But it isn't necessary to go to such lengths. Much simpler counting systems can be devised to give the player an edge under actual casino conditions which are easier to keep accurately and perform almost as well as a hypothetical perfect system. The precise system that is used is comparatively unimportant. The requirements for success are that the player counts accurately, converts the count correctly to estimate the advantage he enjoys, and bets and plays accordingly.

The most important condition, of course, is that *the player is allowed to continue playing.*

No one appreciated this more than Lawrence Revere. Indeed, his main contribution to the game proved to be, not the various counting systems he invented, but rather the techniques he devised to avoid detection. They were so successful that for more than quarter of a century, between the 1950s and his death from cancer at the age of 61 in 1977, he was able to win substantial sums of money from the casinos of Nevada and the West Indies playing the game.

In 1969, Revere published one of the classics of blackjack literature, *Playing Blackjack as a Business*. In this book, he explained the scientific principles of the game with the aid of extensive coloured charts which made use of the computer simulations of Julian Braun. This best-selling book was described in the publisher's blurb as

the first book written by someone who has been a successful blackjack player. The author has spent more time playing blackjack, more time in casinos, and more time in research, than all of the others combined who have written blackjack books or devised blackjack systems.

For once, the hype is justified. Revere died a millionaire; there are few indeed who have succeeded in extracting a million dollars from the casino industry and keeping it. In *Playing Blackjack as a Business*, Revere provides us with a few clues on how he did it and how he was able to go on winning for so long without being barred.

Edward Thorp and his friends drew attention to themselves simply by virtue of the level of stakes for which they played. Even today, thirty years on and with the real value of a dollar severely eroded by inflation, anyone playing for stakes of between $50 and $500 a hand is likely to be closely watched by casino personnel. At a level of $500 a hand, a player who is on a run of luck could make serious inroads into a casino's profitability.

By contrast, Revere played for stakes which did not threaten the casino's profitability. In his view, there was no sense in killing the goose that laid the golden egg; the name of the game was to squeeze as many golden eggs out of the goose as possible without attracting undue attention.

He developed an almost invisible persona:

Perhaps you have a mental picture of a professional gambler, the riverboat stereotype, for example, or the Mafia-type image. You would not recognize me, however, because it is my purpose to be as inconspicuous as possible. I dress as the average customer dresses, and I move into the casino as quietly as I can. When I sit down at a blackjack table I continue to avoid attention in any manner. I purposely play foolishly sometimes to prevent being spotted as a counter, and I occasionally even go so far as to lose bets deliberately . . . I am cold blooded. I play to win. I will only play under the best playing conditions, and then for no more than one hour in a single club. I never sit down at a table with more than two players.

Always play within your bankroll, using no more than a percentage of it as a playing stake. Betting scared money is bad gambling. I use one other cardinal rule: I do not drink when I work, because drinking and playing is like a diamond cutter getting all boozed up and trying to cut a diamond. You will want to be at your very best in order to use the advantages shown to you in this book . . . You will not be gambling when you have learned the advantages set forth in this book. You will be in business.

With these few sentences, a new stereotype began to form of the card counter. He (always a man, never a woman) would be a quiet, deliberate individual, who would concentrate intently on each of the cards dealt. He would not socialize with other players; his object was not entertainment, but profit. He would move from casino to casino unobserved, like the Scarlet Pimpernel.

It is hard work becoming a successful blackjack player. If your count is not perfect, you can make a mistake playing the hands or betting your money. If you do not have the playing strategy down perfectly, you may make a mistake in betting your money, or lose the count. With the ten count strategy, you should win two or three more bets than you lose in each hour that you play. If you make two mistakes an hour, you are not going to win anything.

And so was born the myth of the card counter, as a quiet, intense, anti-social individual.

We find another account of Lawrence Revere's techniques in Humble and Cooper's *The World's Greatest Blackjack Book*. In this book, Lance Humble (a Professor of Psychology at Toronto University whose real name is Igor Kusyshyn) relates how he sought to become Revere's apprentice. One of his students brought a copy of *Playing Blackjack as a Business* to the university class one day, and Humble was sufficiently impressed to seek out Revere on his next trip to Las Vegas.

You can imagine my excitement as I stood at his door about to meet this famous author and gambling expert. When the door opened to my knock, I was momentarily left speechless. I had pictured this man as looking something like Tyrone Power in *The Mississippi Gambler*. Instead, I found a diminutive, freckle-faced little man dressed in a faded blue shirt and wrinkled trousers.

However, despite his unprepossessing appearance, Humble took lessons from Revere and returned to him on later visits.

What kind of man was Lawrence Revere? Most either loved him or hated him. To many casinos, he was barred as a '4'. (Casinos rate players on a 1-to-4 scale: 1 = good, 2 = acceptable, 3 = undesirables such as counters, 4 = cheater). Revere used to be a dealer and knew lots of casino people. He was very good at being able to make deals to cheat casinos. On the other hand, he would sometimes work with casinos in identifying which players were counters. Revere was ruthless in a physically harmless sort of way. He would never hurt you physically. All he wanted was all of your money. He once told me, 'It doesn't matter who wins or loses, only who ends up with the money.' The concept of cheating didn't apply to Revere, because the game he was playing had no rules.

By Humble's account, Revere took on the casinos on their own terms. He was ruthless and amoral, and had no compunction in cheating his fellow gamblers either. For such an individual, the end justified the means – and the end was to win as much money as possible, as quickly as possible.

Fellow gamblers mixed with him at their peril, as Humble was to discover. Humble relates how he and a friend formed a 'partnership' with Revere. They agreed to bankroll him to the tune of two thousand dollars to play in a private game of blackjack, with the profits to be split at the end of the evening.

As the evening progressed, Revere's bankroll was going up and down. About two hours into the game, he motioned me into the bathroom. He told me that he needed more money because he was losing. I was reluctant to give him any more. Suddenly he pulled the 5 of hearts and the 5 of clubs out of his pocket and threw them from the window to the street below. He said that he took the 5s out of the deck and that we were going to have a great advantage now. I watched the two 5s floating down and agreed that it was a beautiful sight. With the larcenous heart of the typical sucker, I gave him another five hundred dollars.

It will be noted that the technique that Revere used to draw his victim deeper into his web was a classic psychological ploy used by charlatans through the ages. He first flattered the hapless Humble by showing him the two 5s – the 5s are the best cards to remove from the deck from the player's point of view, and Revere implicitly acknowledged Humble's expertise by leaving this fact unstated. He also made Humble an accessory to the fraud. The two of them now possessed valuable insider information denied to the other participants in the game.

Of course, the fact that Humble was in on the fraud meant he could hardly complain subsequently if things did not go according to plan. Needless to say, they did not. Three hours later, the partners quit the game and Revere disappeared for a while on the pretext of going to buy cigarettes. When he returned he informed his two partners that he had lost over $2,000 of their money during the evening's play.

I was shocked. I was very surprised that Revere didn't have any more money because I had been watching the game from behind him for the whole evening and it didn't appear that he lost at all. I had figured he broke even. We later found out that he *didn't* lose that much. The people dealing the game told us Revere lost about $250. We suspect that Revere hid the extra money somewhere on his person when he went in to buy cigarettes.

Once stung, Humble did not let Revere handle any more of his money again. However, other people were not so wise, and Humble learnt that Revere's other 'partnerships' also ended with mysteriously high losses. He also relates how Revere fixed private games in which he participated by bringing in card mechanics who were able to manipulate the deal in Revere's favour. Humble ends his account ruefully.

None the less, I have to admit that knowing Revere was worthwhile. Revere was a truly professional gambler – he let nothing stand in his way of getting money. From Revere I learned that gambling could be a ruthless, no-holds-barred profession, and I had the dubious privilege of seeing an expert practice his craft. This kind of gambling is not for me.

Yet even a man with Revere's cold professionalism only played with a tiny edge against the casinos. On Revere's own admission, his expected win rate was a mere two or three bet units an hour. Even that expectation would be destroyed by the tiniest of errors in counting, betting or playing. Furthermore, very few card counters possess Revere's self-discipline and dedication to the game, bordering on the obsessive.

One of the most astonishing details of *Playing Blackjack as a Business* is Revere's own record of six months' play starting on 1 January 1963. This record shows that he played blackjack for 190 consecutive days, keeping

a detailed record of each day's play. During that period, he won a total
of $22,265, with a monthly win ranging from a high of $4,970 in January
1963 to a low of $1,200, in March 1963. That was in much easier
conditions than pertain today, against single-deck games.

If this was all that could be achieved by a player of the ability and
dedication of Lawrence Revere, what serious threat would be posed to
the casinos by less competent card counters playing under much tougher
conditions? The answer is, of course, none whatsoever, *provided* that,
like Revere, they were prepared to grind away for small stakes, hour
after hour, using a modest bet spread and betting no more than, say, $10
a hand.

The real threat comes from the high rollers. The casinos' big profits
come from gamblers who would not flinch at losing several thousand
dollars in a couple of hours. These are the people who could also make
a nasty dent into a casino's profits if they got lucky. Not surprisingly,
therefore, the attention of casino personnel is focused on such players.

The professional card counter was slowly being squeezed out of the
casinos by the 1970s. On the one hand, even counting and playing
perfectly, the best blackjack players in the world could expect to win
only two or three bet units an hour. Playing for $5 a hand, this equated
to an hourly win of only $10 or $15. It was hardly worth the effort. On
the other hand, a counter playing for high stakes – say, $25 a hand, going
up to $100 in favourable situations – would be closely scrutinized by
casino personnel.

In order to win stakes of any consequence, a player would have to try
something different, a new method of play which would not lead to
instant barring.

Ian Andersen was the pseudonym of a high-rolling card counter who
described one such method in his book *Turning the Tables on Las Vegas*
(1976). He analysed the characteristics that typified counter behaviour in
the eyes of the casino – and then devised an act that was the exact
opposite. Andersen described the behaviour pattern of a card counter as
follows:

His demeanour at the table is one of utmost concentration. Meticulously, he
watches each card as he counts. If the pace of the game is slow, he will study the
cards again, just to be absolutely certain he hasn't erred in his count. His betting
is deliberate, calculated. He handles his chips in a polished manner and stacks
them in needy organized, regular piles. Fearful that the dealer will shuffle the
cards in a favourable situation, the counter will often wait until the last possible

moment to place his bet, then quickly make a big bet just before receiving his cards. This often agitates, if not angers, the dealer. When approached by a pit boss, the counter withdraws into his shell. He acts as though he is doing something illegal, arousing the suspicion of the pit boss. He avoids eye contact and begins to fidget. Many idiosyncrasies become apparent as his anxiety increases.

Andersen had learned early in his career that such behaviour was almost a cast-iron guarantee for being barred. To survive in the green baize jungle, effective camouflage was essential.

You can only be a counter if you don't *seem* like one. Be as relaxed and casual as possible. Walk directly to the seat of your choice and sit down. Immediately engage the dealer in conversation. Phrases like 'How have you been running?' or 'Did you just start working?' break the ice. Make eye contact, smile and be pleasant. Small talk and cordiality are disarming. Don't handle your chips efficiently. It is preferable to appear awkward, especially in the presence of a pit boss. Consult him frequently on the play of difficult hands. Give him the impression that he is the expert. Where he gives you advice, tend to follow it even if it's wrong.

Andersen's book is a fascinating insight into the psychology of casino gambling. By Andersen's own account, he was never barred from a Nevada casino once he appreciated that he could only win if he could disguise his expertise. In order to do so, he acted like a high roller, to whom thousands of dollars represented little more than small change. He chatted with casino personnel; tipped liberally and irrationally; seemed to be having a good time when he was winning – 'most counters never change their facial expressions, win or lose'; appeared superstitious when experiencing exceptionally good or bad runs of luck; and frequently played with female partners. He even bought gifts for the casino employees.

All this made him appear like a wealthy playboy, enjoying the casino atmosphere for the entertainment it brought him. In truth, he was playing with cool logic and concealing the extent of his win by pocketing chips as he played while changing more cash into chips. He had learned that a continual flow of cash across the blackjack table was the paramount requirement to keep the pit bosses happy.

All this takes not only a considerable amount of nerve, but also a high degree of concentration. Remember that while Andersen was acting in this way, he was simultaneously counting the cards and adjusting his bet and his playing strategy in an apparently random fashion. Not surprisingly, he, like Lawrence Revere, recommended playing for no longer than 45 minutes in order to keep mentally alert. He also recommended playing with no more than one other player at the table, and preferably alone.

I have nothing but admiration for Andersen's comprehension of the psychology of casino blackjack, and the techniques he used to turn it to his advantage. For many players it is likely to prove difficult to put on such an accomplished act as Andersen's. Even so, within whatever an individual's limitations are, Andersen's advice to act naturally and to establish a rapport with casino personnel remains sound.

The King of Blackjack

There has been an explosive growth in blackjack over the last 30 years, since the publication of *Beat the Dealer*. It is now the most popular casino game in the world. In the 1989 *International Casino Guide*, blackjack is listed as being offered by well over a thousand casinos in more than 80 countries worldwide. These include casinos in every major town and holiday resort in Britain; Nevada and New Jersey in the United States (several other states are expected to legalize the game in the near future); Monte Carlo; throughout the Bahamas and the Caribbean; in Latin America; in virtually every country in Europe, both east and west; in luxury hotels throughout the continents of Africa and Australia; and in Macau and other states in the Far East. The game is also offered at sea on luxury cruise liners. Blackjack is a game with truly international appeal, played by people of all classes and races in every continent. It is possible to play blackjack in elegant casinos from Mayfair to Marrakesh; from Cannes to Kathmandu; or from Baden-Baden to Baghdad.

It seems safe to say that more money is lost at the blackjack tables than in any other social or sporting event.

Blackjack players can be divided into four main groups.

Social players make up by far the largest group, defined not by the sums of money for which they play – which may run into several hundreds of pounds a hand, particularly in the most exclusive Mayfair casinos – but rather by their style. They play according to their hunches, with scant regard to the probabilities in the game. There is little consistency or logic in their play. One common characteristic of social players is that they tend to draw too little – for example, they may stand on 15 or 16 against a dealer's 7 or ace, because they know they are likely to bust if they draw. What they fail to appreciate is that, mathematically, they would expect to lose less by drawing than by standing, because of the high probability that the dealer will draw to a hand of between 17 and 21 and so beat any total less than 17. Because they make incorrect plays of this type, social players are at a serious disadvantage to the casinos, with a negative expectation of between −1 per cent and −5 per cent.

The second group, which comprises less than 10 per cent of all players, possesses some rudimentary knowledge of the probabilities of the game, and plays to something approximating basic strategy. They play under a disadvantage of approximately 1 per cent against the casino.

The third group comprises players who try to count the cards as they are dealt, and adjust their bet and play accordingly – maybe one or two out of every one hundred players. However, not all of these players have an edge over the casino. They may count inaccurately, or overbet a limited bankroll, and are consequently likely to lose over a long series of plays.

The final group consists of those players who are able to gain an edge over the casino by card counting, and win consistently.

Even for a card-counting player, favourable situations arise infrequently. Waiting for them requires immense patience, since they will occur for less than 15 per cent of the time in a typical four-deck game, or for less than ten minutes in an average hour of play. The remainder of the time is spent waiting, and keeping count of the cards as they are dealt. Very few players possess the dedication, concentration and self-discipline necessary to beat the game. On the basis of my own observations over many hundred hours, I would guess that less than one in a thousand players of the game win consistently. My library is filled with books boasting such titles as *Blackjack – Your Way to Riches*, *Blackjack Super Gold*, *Winning Blackjack Made Easy* and *Million Dollar Blackjack*. These titles are misleading. Blackjack is emphatically *not* a quick and easy way to riches. A winning player faces a long, hard, lonely grind; and he or she must learn to accept that the final product of all this effort may not be riches but ruin. Casinos worldwide make well over $1,000 million every year from the blackjack tables; they do not do so dealing to winning players.

The tiny minority of winning players are overwhelmingly male. Because the casinos know this, and because many of their executive staff tend to be chauvinist, any lady who learnt how to count and play accurately would enjoy a considerable advantage over a man with equivalent skills. She would be permitted to go on playing longer, and with wider bet spreads, than a male card counter.

One of the rare occasions I have come across a lady card counter was in a small casino in a coastal resort in south-west England. Though I did not speak to her, in the quarter of an hour during which she was playing at the same table I was able to deduce that she was probably using a one-level card count; that she did not adjust the running count according to the number of cards that had been dealt; and that she did not adjust her playing strategy away from the basic strategy according to the proportion of high or low cards remaining. I therefore concluded that, although she appeared to be a competent card counter, her win rate was likely to be very small and was probably negative.

The problem of how to escape the unwelcome attentions of the pit bosses is one that continues to vex card counters. Probably the most successful solution to date was devised by Ken Uston, the uncrowned King of Blackjack. Uston was the most famous blackjack player of the 1970s and 1980s, a flamboyant self-publicist whose photographs often show him with a bottle of champagne in one hand and a blonde in the other as he celebrates yet another big win. He probably approximates the traditional image of a Mississippi riverboat gambler more closely than any of the other great players of the game.

A man of high intelligence who had graduated from the University of Yale and Harvard Business School, he arrived at the blackjack tables by way of the Pacific Stock Exchange. Before he renounced finance for gambling, Ken Uston had risen to be a Senior Vice-president of the Pacific Stock Exchange. By the early 1970s, he was earning $50,000 a year – equivalent to well over $100,000 in today's money. He renounced this successful and secure existence when he learnt how blackjack could be beaten from a gambler whom he identifies simply as Al Francesco. Between the early 1970s and the late 1980s, Uston made his living from blackjack.

It was not the comfortable or glamorous existence some might imagine, as Ken Uston revealed in an interview with Arnold Snyder in *Blackjack Forum*:

When we started playing back in 1973, the casinos treated us like criminals. Sure, we were making a lot of money and we were making very high bets. But the point is we were treated like crooks. We were trailed. We were hustled into back rooms. I got my face broken and went into hospital, I guess because the pit boss noticed who I was ... To this day I don't have any feeling in part of my mouth.

Uston played on his own all over the world, but became particularly famous for organizing teams of card-counting blackjack players who would hit selected casinos. Uston played successfully in a number of blackjack teams organized by Al Francesco and others in Las Vegas. His teams operated with extremely high bet spreads, or ratios of bets placed in very favourable situations compared to unfavourable situations. They could achieve such high spreads by placing card counters at different blackjack tables within a casino, who bet the table minimum and played basic strategy while waiting for a favourable situation to arise. They then 'called in' a big player, who might be ambling around chatting to casino personnel and drinking.

The big player was actually watching the counters for a pre-arranged signal undetectable to casino personnel. The signals could include the card counter stroking an ear-lobe or brushing back his hair. Once the signal had been given, the big player would arrive at the blackjack table and place a high bet, which might be as high as the table maximum. Since the player had only just arrived, the casino personnel had no basis for suspecting that he knew the cards were in the player's favour. For all the world he appeared merely to be a high-rolling 'hunch' gambler who just happened to be lucky.

If executed skilfully, such team play was undetectable and, with an adequately capitalized bank, swung the odds of the game decisively in the playing team's favour.

Team play had a number of other advantages. First, since team players were sitting at four or five tables, the big player was able to place big bets in four or five times as many favourable situations as an individual card counter. This advantage was compounded by the fact that the team could achieve a far greater bet spread than any individual player, since the big player did not appear to be spreading his bets at all, but merely placing consistently high bets: Uston states that his teams often achieved an effective spread of 40 or 50 to 1, which would be impossible for any individual to achieve undetected. Moreover, because the big player played many times more favourable shoes than an individual, the fluctuations in the team's bankroll was proportionately less than the fluctuations in any individual's bankroll would have been. When negative fluctuations did occur, the presence of a team lent moral and psychological support to alleviate the intense loneliness that an individual player can experience when things are running against him.

There can be disadvantages to team play. A blackjack team is a partnership, and like any partnership depends on trust between the partners, which can break down when things are going badly. This is particularly likely if certain team members are suspected of not pulling their weight: for example, missing the count, or sending the wrong signals or, worst of all, suspected of theft from the team's bank.

It should be emphasized that team play does not guarantee a win. A team's bankroll can be wiped out just as an individual's can if there is a negative deviation from the expected result. But if correctly applied with an adequate bankroll, team play can generate substantial profits.

Uston's first team broke up with a profit of $500,000 split among twenty players. His second team grossed $650,000. His third team, which used a computer, was rapidly identified and barred. His fourth team lost $139,000, which Uston put down to errors caused by over-elaborate signalling between the counters and the big player. The team did not get the opportunity to win that money back.

Word was out that we were around – we'd been working in town (Las Vegas) for nearly a year. By the fall of 1978, we found it virtually impossible to get a good game. We worked with some known high-rolling losers, which was successful for a while. They'd put up the money and we'd supply the counting ability – we'd split the win. But the games kept deteriorating and eventually Team 4 broke up.

At that point, Ken Uston proceeded to Atlantic City.

Until 1978, Nevada had been the only state of the USA where casino gambling was legal. However, in a 1976 referendum, the citizens of New Jersey had approved the legalization of casino gambling in Atlantic City by a 2–1 majority, and on 26 May 1978 the first Atlantic City casino, Resorts International, opened its doors.

The casino was granted a temporary nine-month licence. It was clear from the outset that the casino would be a commercial success, tapping a huge latent demand for casino gambling in the north-eastern states of the USA. According to Chambliss and Roginski's authoritative work, *Playing Blackjack in Atlantic City*, the gross profits of Resorts International averaged $600,000 *per day*, or over $4 million per week, by the early 1980s. Three other casinos were opened in 1979 and 1980, and their combined weekly gross profit amounted to $2 million a day or $14 million a week by the early 1980s.

Harder times were to follow when the casino owners led by Donald Trump over-expanded in the late 1980s, financing further casino developments with high-interest debt. However, in 1978/9, with only one casino in operation, demand far exceeded supply, and there were frequently queues of gamblers waiting for a seat to become available at the blackjack tables.

During the nine-month temporary licence period which ran from May 1978 to February 1979, Resorts International did not bar card counters. This provided a unique opportunity for Ken Uston and the other professional card counters to play. The rules of the game were so liberal that a basic strategy player, playing perfectly while betting a flat amount on each hand, enjoyed a small edge against the casino. For example, one of the options offered was the highly advantageous 'surrender' option, whereby a player could opt to give up his hand for the forfeit of one-half of the bet placed. This option originated in Macao in the Far East, but is now offered by very few casinos. It is similar to throwing in a poker hand and can considerably reduce the player's losses on poor hands such as hard 16 against a dealer's ace which the player would normally expect to lose.

Over the next few months there ensued one of the most bizarre episodes in the history of gambling as a 'counter convention' took place in Atlantic City. During this period individual card counters and teams from all over the world openly took on Resorts International.

The most flamboyant among them was Ken Uston, who estimated that in January 1979 alone card counters won about $1 million from Resorts. Despite this, Resorts was still grossing some $20 million profit per month, so even this intense effort by the world's greatest blackjack players was not enough to make much of a dent in casino profitability. It seems likely that the liberality of the rules at the blackjack tables attracted far more losing than winning players, so that it might have been in the casinos' commercial interest to continue offering liberal rules and tolerate the minority of winning card counters who played at the tables.

Needless to say, this was not the option chosen by Resorts. It wanted the right to eliminate the winners and deal only to mugs with more money than sense.

On January 30, Commission Chairman Joseph Lordi allowed Resorts to bar 'professional card counters' and the Counters' Convention ended. Through lawyer Morris Goldings, I filed a complaint with the Commission, challenging their right to bar any players solely on the basis of their skill.

Ken Uston's Newsletters on Blackjack, 1979–1981

The action now shifts from the blackjack tables to the law courts. Initially Uston's appeal was successful.

On October 24, 1979, the New Jersey Gaming Commission agreed to proceed with an experiment whereby the rules of blackjack would be made tougher and all players, regardless of skill level, would be allowed to play.

Ken Uston's Newsletters on Blackjack, 1979–1981

The experiment began on 1 December 1979. As Uston's *Newsletters* make clear, he felt from the outset that the casinos were exaggerating the threat caused by card counters, and were not entering the experiment in good faith. In addition, Uston argued that the tougher conditions were costing the casinos more in terms of lost profits from ordinary gamblers than they were saving from card counters. Uston's *Newsletter* of December 1979 set out his reasoning:

From the start, the Commission was supplied inaccurate data from the casinos on amounts won by counters. After four days, one team, which started with a $40,000 bank, went broke. Most other teams were either in the red or at break-even. Yet casino profits were down significantly, and I doubted that these figures were doctored. I attributed the decrease in profitability to two factors:

1 The cut card was now at half the shoe, rather than at one-third, as previously. We clocked the average number of rounds dealt, which decreased from 55 to 48 rounds per hour, a drop in volume of nearly 13 per cent. Thus on capacity nights blackjack profitability would be expected to drop by 13 per cent, or perhaps $50,000 per day, without the casinos making a nickle.

2 Our team of nine players played real lucky and won far more than expected value in the first week (one player called it 'karma' since we alone had paid the legal fees in the long fight to gain readmittance). We were at 3 or 4 standard deviations to the right.

Despite Ken Uston's reasoning, the Atlantic City experiment ended with a ruling in the casinos' favour. Henceforward, they were allowed to bar professional card counters – which in practice meant anyone they didn't like. With the counters excluded, their profits improved further. In April 1981 according to Uston's *Newsletter* of the following month, the 486 blackjack tables operating in Atlantic City grossed a profit of $18.48 million. Profits were further increased by the elimination of the 'surrender' option in the following month.

Uston continued the process of negotiation and litigation with the casinos throughout the mid-1980s. His objective was to try to agree terms and conditions with the casinos that would permit known card counters to play unmolested, yet be sufficiently strict to ensure that the casinos' overall profitability would not be jeopardized. Among Uston's suggestions was that the casinos would allow only a limited bet spread, of about 1–4 bet units; they would cut no more than one-third of a six-deck shoe out of play; and they would reserve the right to shuffle up if a new player entered the game in the course of the shoe in order to counter the team play from which he himself had made so much money. These conditions would be very difficult for even the most skilful black-jack players to beat. As a quid pro quo, the casinos would undertake to honour a no-barring policy towards card counters.

In mid-1981, the case went to appeal, which Uston won. The day after the decision, Ken Uston returned to the Resorts Casino in triumph.

The verdict was a major defeat for the casinos, which have already barred some 1,500 players from the blackjack tables here. Last night Uston returned to the scene of the original crime. He said he didn't go to rub salt in the wound, just to splash it with a little champagne. Surrounding him in Resorts' Rendezvous Lounge were three bottles of champagne, two beautiful women and several re-porters and photographers. Uston seemed drunk on the potent tonic of victory. 'I wonder how much Resorts spent in legal fees,' mused Uston, who himself spent nearly $30,000 pressing the suit. 'It must have been in six figures. Why didn't they just let me play blackjack for it? To give it to their attorney instead of me just doesn't seem right.'

Atlantic City Press, 12 May 1981

However, Ken's moment of triumph was not to last. Encouraged by his entourage, he made his way to a $25 blackjack table and won the first hand. It was also to be his last.

Nervous consultations began among supervisors in the pit and an apologetic floorman approached Uston and said, 'Mr Uston, the paperwork hasn't come through yet. You can't play.' Uston laughed and stood up. He tossed the $25 chip he had just won to the dealer, saying, 'For the boys.'

The casinos took the case to the Supreme Court of New Jersey. In an interview with Arnold Snyder in *Blackjack Forum* two years later, Ken Uston recollected how the casinos had spent between half a million and a million dollars on legal and consultancy fees in the case. The case for the card counters was knocked together by Uston himself just before the hearing was due to commence. 'I took a little portable typewriter and typed a list of proposals outside the men's room of Howard Johnson's. And that was the counter's side. A piece of paper prepared in 45 minutes.'

The ultimate result was inevitable. Despite Uston's minor victories along the way, the ultimate decision was in favour of the casinos. They were given the right to bar card counters, a right they maintain to this day.

Yes, I was bitter. I felt an equilibrium (between the players and the casinos) had been achieved, but the 'tap-dancing' of the casino people prevented it from being implemented. I vowed to redouble our legal efforts to effect a no-barring policy in New Jersey. We left town.

Million Dollar Blackjack

Ken Uston concluded his account of the New Jersey experiment as follows:

Permitting barring effectively grants casino personnel the privilege of excluding just about anyone they want, under the guise of being 'professionals'. Photographing, surveillance and harassment of persons suspected of being skilful is the result. A general atmosphere of suspicion, unfriendliness and resentment between casino personnel and players is fostered, as floormen monitor players' behaviour to determine their playing ability and casino security guards are called upon to eject players.

It would appear that a more sensible solution to this problem lies in exactly what the (New Jersey) commission attempted. That is, establishing blackjack conditions that do not work to the disadvantage of the general public, but which still eliminate a significant portion of the skilled player's statistical advantage over the house.

This, combined with a no-barring policy, will create an 'open environment', where the skilled blackjack player and the pit boss will not be placed in adversarial positions. A positive, healthy atmosphere will be created, in which, just as with chess, backgammon and bridge, skill at blackjack will be viewed with respect.

Million Dollar Blackjack

Sadly, Ken Uston is no longer with us to argue this case. He passed away in a Paris hotel while on vacation in October 1987. He was found in bed with his hands behind his head as if in deep reflection. At the time of his death, he was fifty-two years old. I hope he went peacefully. He left the world of gambling a heritage of adventures and ideas on blackjack in the many books and articles he published. Despite his sometimes irritating penchant for self-publicity, he remains a hero of mine.

For his contributions to the theory of blackjack – including the Uston advanced point count, one of the most accurate card-counting systems ever devised; for the exuberance with which he played the game and chronicled his adventures; for his dignity in defeat and his generosity in victory; and, above all, for his courage in taking on the might of the Nevada and Atlantic City casinos on the tables and in the law courts, at some physical and financial risk to himself – for all these things, for me, Kenny Uston remains the greatest blackjack player of them all.

Blackjack in the 1980s and 1990s

Since the New Jersey experiment of the early 1980s, the battle between the casinos and card-counting players has settled into an unstable equilibrium. The mathematical principles by which the game can be beaten are well established and are known to serious gamblers and casino executives alike. The casinos themselves make substantial profits from the game, indicating that they have largely neutralized any threat posed by skilful players. Yet Ken Uston's dream of conditions under which skilful players will be allowed to participate freely in the game remains unfulfilled.

Every time a skilful blackjack player takes on the casinos, a battle takes place between the individual and the system. On one side is the player, totally on his own, with a limited bankroll and only his wits as a weapon to gain the tiniest of edges in the game. On the other side are the casinos. They decide the rules and the conditions under which the game is played. They determine which individuals are allowed to participate. Any individuals they suspect of being capable of winning consistently will be barred.

An exception to the barring rule exists in Canada, where the Province of Alberta's Gaming Control Section has issued the following policy statement:

Card counters who obtain an honest advantage over the house through a playing strategy do not break any law . . . Gaming supervisors should ensure that no steps are taken to discourage any player simply because he is winning.

There are no signs of British gaming authorities following this enlightened lead.

In his book *The Blackjack Formula* (1980), Arnold Snyder set out a methodology by which a player could establish whether a game could be mathematically beaten, and if so what bet spread would be required. He concluded his analysis with the words.

The days may be numbered for professional card counters. If the Blackjack Formula offers nothing else, it will at least offer the professional a means of determining when that number is up.

Things may not be quite as grim for the gambler as this implies. As long as blackjack is offered by casinos, no matter how poor the rules or conditions, you can rest assured that someone somewhere will be dreaming up a new idea to gain an edge over it.

Arnold Snyder is right to emphasize that the margin between success and failure at blackjack is a very fine one. Even when the player's mathematical expectation is positive there is no guarantee that the player will win. Given an expected statistical variance of possible outcomes, even a skilful player who counts accurately, bets prudently and plays correctly will experience the depressing experience of losing a series of large bets one after another. It is far, far easier to lose money playing casino blackjack than it is to win (I speak from painful experience). Winning requires intense concentration, nerves of steel, and a large bankroll. Given the choice, I would place my wager on the dealer every time. Unfortunately, this choice is not offered by the casinos. We are left with no alternative but to use every available means to maximize the player's chances of success, and to avoid situations which could erode the player's potential edge.

The most obvious factor that could erode the skilful player's edge is cheating by the dealer. The player's edge is little more than 1 per cent even under the most favourable conditions. A winning player could expect to win a maximum of 3 or 4 bet units over 100 hands of play from bets totalling 300 bet units. If a dealer was somehow able to deal the cards so as to be certain of winning just one of the player's large bets, the player's edge would be destroyed completely.

I believe there is little, if any, cheating by the casinos in Britain. There may be a few individual *dealers* who cheat without the knowledge of the casino management, but even this would be extremely rare and difficult to execute. It is not in the interests of casinos to cheat; they have too much to lose. Casinos in Britain are run by reputable companies, many publicly owned and quoted on the Stock Exchange, under the supervision of the government-appointed Gaming Board. If it was proved that a casino was cheating its customers, not only would that casino lose its licence (and its employees be thrown out of work) but the reputation of the company owning it would suffer immense damage.

The same applies to individual dealers and pit bosses who might be tempted to cheat without the knowledge of the senior management of the casino. All casino employees have to be licensed by the Gaming Board, and any individual found guilty of cheating would have his or her licence revoked and not be able to work in the casino industry again.

Nevertheless, given the potential rewards from cheating a high roller in a large casino, there may be individual dealers who could be tempted to take that risk, particularly if they were colluding with another player or an inspector to extract money from the casino.

The most obvious method would be to strip a deck of 10s, court cards or aces. This would swing the mathematical odds further in the casino's favour. But it would be very difficult to strip a deck undetected. Before the start of play, all four decks used in a game are laid face up for inspection by the first players and a casino inspector to ensure they are complete. Thereafter, dealers at a table are changed every twenty minutes or half hour.

It would be just possible for a dealer to remove some cards if a table was temporarily empty and the pit boss's attention distracted. But the risks would be enormous, and it is difficult to envisage a dealer getting away with it under pit boss and video surveillance on more than one or two occasions.

A more subtle and less risky method of cheating would be for the dealer to shuffle the cards to ensure that the shoe would favour the dealer rather than the player as it was dealt out. The shoe would be complete but the conformation of the cards would favour the dealer.

I witnessed Darwin Ortiz, a leading American authority on gambling scams, demonstrate a number of false shuffles which would favour the dealer at a presentation in London in August 1990. This demonstration confirmed the results of computer simulations of shuffles which indicate that it is extremely difficult to achieve a genuinely random shuffle, and that there are certain types of shuffle which can considerably enhance the edge a casino enjoys over the player. It has been suggested that such shuffles have been employed by certain casinos in practice.

In his excellent technical primer, *A Book on Casino Blackjack*, C. Ionescu Tulcea cites the following experiment with a stacked deck:

Stacking means setting the cards in a pre-determined order. A 'popular' method of stacking, disadvantageous for the player when he is alone at the table, consists of arranging the cards in low-high or high-low order. It is not necessary that all the cards be arranged in low-high or high-low order. For the player to be at a disadvantage it is enough that the pack contains one or more such sequences ... The dealer has an additional advantage (of knowing whether the next card is likely to be high or low). Hence, if he wants a low card he will deal the next one. If he wants a high card he will deal a second.

The following experiment is of interest: a 52–card deck was divided into two parts, denoted L and H respectively. In L we put all the low cards plus two 8s and in H all the high cards plus two 8s. The deck was set at random in low-high order. The player bet one unit on each hand. The number of units lost or won by the player was recorded.

The experiment was repeated through 500 decks. The same type of experiment was repeated, also 500 times, with the deck set in high-low order. The results were the following:

In the case where the decks were set in low-high order the player lost a total of 1,710 units.

In the case where decks were set in high-low order the player lost a total of 1,130 units.

Observe that in both cases the player's losses were very large. This is quite impressive since, in one-deck games played under basic rules, the basic strategy player is not at a disadvantage. We conclude that the low-high and high-low stackings are devastating for the player.

Similar results could be achieved by other shuffles, or by the dealer dealing a 'second' to favour himself or hurt the player. Although dealing seconds from a shoe is more difficult than from a hand-held game, it is by no means impossible. Nor is the ability to do so limited to theatrical magicians.

The only way in which such cheating could be detected is by collating a large number of statistics on the game over an extended period. In *The Theory of Blackjack*, Professor Peter Griffin cited a number of occasions on which he was cheated:

I had been moderately successful playing until the pendulum swung. Trying to discover some reason for Dame Fortune's fick'eness, I embarked upon a lengthy observation of the frequency of dealer-up cards in the casinos I had suffered most in. The result of my sample, that the dealers had 770 10s (including court cards) or aces out of 1820 hands played, was a statistically significant indication of some sort of legerdemain.

It would be possible for a player to establish whether the dealer was receiving favourable cards more often than he or she should, by observing the outcome of a large number of hands, and calculating the probability of the outcome.

Thus, in the example cited by Professor Griffin, the dealer would *expect* to draw an ace or 10 as the first card 700 times in 1820 hands. The fact that the dealer exceeded that expectation by 70, or 10 per cent, is not of itself surprising. What is surprising is the number of standard deviations that represents. The standard deviation of the expected number of 10s or aces among 1820 cards dealt is 20.75, calculated by methods described in Appendix I. For 99.7 per cent of the time, the actual result *should* fall within three standard deviations of the expected result, or (20.75 × 3) = ± 62.25. The result observed by Professor Griffin lies *above* the maximum limit of the range, and thus constitutes a 0.3 per cent chance only. In other words, it represents an event that would be expected to occur on less than one out of every 300 deals of 1820 cards. The Professor's suspicions therefore appear well founded.

The example demonstrates the sort of analysis that would have to be undertaken to check on the probability of dealer cheating. Such an analysis would require many hours of play.

A more practical method is for the player to stop playing and leave the table if the dealer seems to be winning an unusually high number of hands, or receiving a lot of aces and 10s as the first card. In all likelihood the dealer is merely experiencing a run of good fortune; but why take the risk that he or she may be the helping odds along by some underhand means?

Another threat to a player's success is posed by the accident of a dealer's bias. A dealer's bias occurs when the running count rises as a shoe is dealt out, and goes on rising as more and more small cards are dealt. The higher cards which favour the player are never dealt *because they are located behind the cut card.* That particular shoe exhibits a bias in favour of the dealer, because the cards that are actually dealt favour the dealer. The cut card is reached and the shoe is shuffled before the high cards favouring the player can be dealt.

A dealer's bias will occur from time to time as a result of the random distribution of the cards after a shuffle. There is, of course, an equal chance of a player's bias arising after a shuffle. A player's bias is the exact reverse of a dealer's bias: high cards are dealt out, while the low cards remain behind the cut card. In this case, the player usually wins more hands than the dealer, and benefits by drawing high cards on doubled bets. Meanwhile, the running count turns negative, and gets progressively lower as the shoe goes on.

While the two biases are equally likely, their effect on the card counter differs greatly. If the card count turns negative off the top of the shoe, a card counter will place a low bet. He is likely to win more hands than he will lose, but unfortunately the bets he wins will be small ones.

By contrast, if the card count becomes positive, the card counter will start to increase his bet. If there is a dealer's bias, small cards will be dealt out, the count will go higher and higher and the card counter will place larger and larger bets. But those bets won't win. Low cards will continue to be dealt out and the dealer will be unlikely to bust. The high cards that the player expects to see remain stubbornly behind the cut card.

The importance of these considerations led to the development of techniques for tracking the shuffle during the 1980s. It occurred to a number of gamblers that, just as the dealer may shuffle the cards to gain an edge, so the player may follow the cards as they are shuffled to identify where in the shoe he or she would expect to find a predominance of high or low cards.

The development of blackjack theory has undergone four distinct phases since mathematical methods of analysis were first applied to it in the 1950s. The first phase, during the 1950s, saw the calculation of the basic strategy for the game by the Baldwin group in the United States. The second phase began with the publication of *Beat the Dealer*, which demonstrated how the game could be beaten by means of card counting. During the decade following the publication of *Beat the Dealer*, techniques for counting the cards were revised and developed. However, as the casinos became aware of these techniques, they took measures to counter them and neutralize the threat posed by skilful players. The third phase of blackjack's development saw students of the game analysing ways in which a player could gain an edge under the restrictive conditions offered by the casinos in the 1970s and 1980s. The most effective method was through the formation of teams of professional blackjack players, of which the most famous were those of the late Ken Uston.

But by the early 1980s, the casinos had got wind of such techniques and new methods of beating the game had to be devised. The technique of shuffle tracking, introduced into blackjack from poker, was the most significant innovation of the fourth phase of blackjack's development.

The concept of shuffle tracking was first published in the August 1983 edition of the American *Gambling Times*. In its simplest form, it entails counting down the cards as they are dealt from the shoe and then keeping track of what happens to the undealt cards located behind the cut card as the shoe is shuffled. More sophisticated methods for tracking the shuffle were described by Jerry Patterson, a close associate of Ken Uston, in books such as *Break the Dealer* and *Blackjack's Winning Formula*. These methods require the player to observe when groups of cards favourable to him are dealt in the course of the shoe and note where they are placed in the discard pile. The player then watches as the dealer shuffles, and cuts these favourable clumps to the top of the new shoe. Thus, even if the cut card is inserted high, the player can place a large bet on the first hand of the new shoe in the confident knowledge that he has an edge over the dealer. This is exactly the opposite of what the casinos would expect a card counter to do.

The ideal situation to execute these techniques is for the player to play head-to-head against the dealer. If other players are at the table, then someone else may pick up the cut card and cut the good (high) cards to the bottom of the shoe.

It is not possible to track all shuffles. As casinos have become aware of the possible threat posed by shuffle tracking, their shuffles have become more complex, making it difficult to follow clumps of cards through the shuffle. Nevertheless, it has been my experience that the shuffle of many dealers can be tracked, particularly at smaller provincial casinos in Britain, and that accurate shuffle tracking can complement conventional card-counting techniques and add usefully to the player's edge.

A second new idea was introduced during the 1980s by the professional player Stanford Wong. It involves not playing at all when the shoe is negative, and only playing after a series of small cards have been dealt out. Two variants of this are 'back counting' (standing behind a blackjack table and only placing a bet when the card count indicates the player has an edge) and 'table hopping' (moving from table to table and placing bets whenever a number of low cards are dealt out at any point during the shoe).

Back counting can be used for short bursts in British casinos but if it is prolonged, it may be noticed by casino personnel and the player will be barred (I was barred from one casino after employing this technique). Table hopping is designed for the large casinos of Las Vegas and Atlantic City, some of which have as many as 60 blackjack tables in operation at peak times; it is clearly not feasible in smaller British casinos with a couple of tables only. Stanford Wong himself claims never to have been barred from an American casino for using the technique, and to earn several thousand dollars a year from it.

A third advance since 1980 has been the more rigorous evaluation of the conditions under which blackjack can be beaten. Much useful work has been done on evaluating playing conditions by Arnold Snyder, who built upon the theoretical work of Professor Griffin to devise what he termed the blackjack formula in 1980. This formula gives an estimate of the player's expected profit for blackjack. It is a complex mathematical equation of uncertain derivation. In a number of subsequent books, including *Blackjack for Profit* and *Beat the Four-deck Game*, Snyder spelt out the practical implications of his formula and calculated the precise conditions under which the skilful player could expect to gain an edge over the dealer. These conditions do not include the efficiency of the particular counting system used. Any of the generally recognized counting systems can in principle enable a good player to gain a winning edge.

He indicates that the single most important factor in determining how easy it is to beat the game is the number of decks used. The best game for a skilful player is the one-deck game. This is not, however, offered in British casinos, which universally play with four-deck shoes.

The second most important factor is the rules of play offered. British rules are not particularly favourable to the player, since they only permit the player to double down on hard totals of 9, 10 or 11, and not to double down on soft totals (that is, totals including an ace which may be valued as either 1 or 11); they only allow insurance of blackjacks; and they do not allow pairs to be re-split. Against these limitations, a player is allowed to double down after splitting a pair if he draws to 9, 10 or 11 on one of the split cards, which is a distinct advantage.

Given that the British game is played from a four-deck shoe with unfavourable rules, the player starts the game with a disadvantage of approximately −0.65 per cent playing basic strategy. With such a start, Snyder's blackjack formula indicates that the game can only be beaten if three conditions hold. First, the player must use a bet spread of at least 8–1 (i.e., place 8 bet units when the true count is high, and 1 bet unit otherwise). Second, at least 75 per cent – and ideally 80 per cent – of the cards in the shoe should be dealt out before the cut card is reached and the cards are shuffled up. Third, there should be no more than one or two other players at the table.

If any of these conditions are not met, the game becomes at best marginal profitable. At worst, with a full table, a cut card inserted only 66 per cent of the way down the shoe, and a bet spread of only 2–1 or 3–1, even the most skilful player is likely to lose in the long run.

Unless the player can get a reasonable bet spread, the profits generated by the few high bets that mostly win will be insufficient to cover the losses sustained on the many low bets that mostly lose. If the cut card is not inserted deep into the shoe of cards, the true count will not rise high enough often enough to make the game worth playing. And if there are too many players at the table, the game just becomes a lottery.

In my experience, one factor outweighs all Snyder's mathematical considerations: the psychology of the gambler. Even competent card counters may lack self-discipline. They play when they are tired and not counting accurately. They refuse to leave when they fall behind, but fall foul of the gambler's worst enemy, steaming, and increase their bets in an attempt to recoup their loses, without regard to the odds and fluctuations of the game. They play in conditions they know intuitively to be unbeatable, where the cut card is inserted high, or where the table is crowded with too many players. They make mistakes in betting and playing. I have been guilty of all of the above.

There are a hundred ways of losing at casino blackjack. There is one, and only one, way of winning: by a long, hard grind, of counting, betting and playing perfectly in games where the conditions of play are good: and accepting that there will be frequent negative fluctuations around the positive expected result.

In blackjack, as in other fields of human endeavour, those who ultimately triumph are not necessarily those with the greatest flair or ability. They are those who adopt what John von Neumann and Oscar Morgenstern termed the minimax principle in their *Theory of Games and Economic Behavior*. The minimax principle is the principle of minimizing the maximum risk, and it is the strategy most likely to result in success in contests of human skill, whether they be wars, games of physical skill such as tennis or football, or mathematical games such as chess or bridge. Spectacular coups which maximize the chances of immediate success, but have a high risk of immediate failure, may please the crowd and give the player a great sense of satisfaction when they come off; but they will not ensure success over a long, closely fought series of trials. At the highest level, in any closely fought contest, the ultimate outcome will depend less on natural flair than on careful and patient assessment of the risks.

The margin between success and failure in blackjack is very fine. In normal circumstances, it favours the house. The house cannot make mistakes because it plays according to a set of specific rules. However, even the house, with the odds weighted in its favour, will suffer negative swings on up to a third of all its blackjack tables, and on perhaps one out of ten occasions these negative swings will be sufficient for the house to lose over a full session of play. Even a casino is vulnerable to a high-rolling gambler on a lucky streak whose win swamps the losses of a number of smaller players. Such a run by the Australian magnate Kerry Packer during a visit to England in 1989 contributed to the downfall of the European Leisure casinos in Mayfair.

If casinos are vulnerable to such fluctuations, with their large bankrolls and wide spread of risk over several tables and many shifts, it is clear that the individual gambler is far more exposed. The individual will have a smaller bankroll, less opportunity to get into the long run and, most crucially, is liable to make mistakes. This is particularly so when the gambler is losing and under increasing psychological pressure.

Each individual must find his own solution to this problem. The easiest solution is, of course, not to gamble at all. Failing this, professional gamblers establish a series of rules for themselves, such as the following:

1   Never play with money you cannot afford to lose. Gambling with scared money is likely to lead to mistakes, particularly on those critical percentage hands such as drawing to a total of between 12 and 16 against a dealer's high up card. The frightened gambler is likely to play too conservatively – for example, standing when he should draw.

2   Never bet more than a certain percentage of your bankroll on any hand, no matter how great the theoretical advantage. Blackjack professionals who rely on the game for their livelihood are unlikely to bet more than 1 per cent of their bankrolls on any single hand; semi-professionals, who are not dependent on the game, may be more aggressive, betting perhaps 2 or 3 per cent of their bankrolls in very favourable situations. Going above these limits carries a high risk of ruin.

3   Only play when you are in peak physical and mental condition and feel relaxed and confident.

4   Do not play in adverse conditions: for example, where the cut card is inserted higher than 75 per cent of the way down the shoe, or where the

dealer is unpleasant or arrogant or seems to be drawing a disproportionate number of tens and aces as his first card.

5   Only play for a specified period of no more than an hour and always set a stop-loss limit. Once this limit has been reached, leave the table to avoid further losses. The best way to avoid the temptation of playing on too long is only to enter the casino with the number of betting units you are prepared to lose, and to leave all other access to cash and credit at home, so that if you are cleaned out you have no option but to get up and leave.

It is still possible to win at casino blackjack, though the techniques have changed. However, it seems doubtful whether any contemporary British player earns the sort of money that the little guy from California, Lawrence Revere or Ken Uston made playing the game. Even Stanford Wong, a highly successful contemporary professional in the United States, probably earns no more than $50,000 a year from blackjack – a reasonable living, but hardly a fortune.

My own playing career was severely curtailed after a playing session at the Golden Nugget in London's Shaftesbury Avenue, during the course of which I lost £400. This occurred on a quiet winter's afternoon, and I learned subsequently from an independent but reliable source that my play had been videotaped and analysed by casino personnel. Within 48 hours I had received letters from the Sportsman, the Palm Beach, and the Casanova casino club – all of which are members of the same group as the Golden Nugget – informing me that my membership of those clubs had been terminated.

The size of the stake is not the issue. A player of my acquaintance was asked to leave a casino after playing for small stakes for less than an hour, having won £15.

When I was barred from the Brent Walker casinos, I concluded that George Walker's business empire was in serious trouble. It was. When Stakis barred me, at a time when I had not been near a Stakis casino for three months, I concluded that a company doctor to the Stakis group would not be far behind. He wasn't.

What I suspect was happening in these groups was the following. In the boom years of the late 1980s, their managements had embarked on ambitious expansion programmes funded largely by debt. When the economy turned in the early 1990s, and interest rates rose, they were left highly exposed and their profits plunged. The pressures were transmitted from the banks and the shareholders, through senior management down to the managers at casino level. Because of the errors made by senior management, the situation could only be retrieved by squeezing greater profits out of the casinos.

By the early 1990s the more sophisticated casino managements, particularly in the United States, began to recognize that they might have more to lose than to gain by barring casual card counters. Having changed the rules and conditions of play to make the game difficult to beat, they realized that their net profits could actually be reduced by barring any suspected counter, because in the process they would also eliminate non-counters who happened to be on a lucky streak and even card counters who could not beat the game in the long run. In addition, as Ken Uston's account of the New Jersey experiment makes clear, the most obvious counter-measure of moving the cut card up the shoe significantly reduces the rate of play, and thus of casino profit.

In a recent interview, Peter Griffin, the world's leading authority on the mathematics of blackjack, said:

I think the American casinos have changed their attitude a little bit. Quite a few people highly placed in casino management recognize that card counting itself cannot really bankrupt a casino in any short period of time. And for any card counter who's competent, there are ten who aren't really competent, and thousands of people who are pouring money over the tables at a rate that not even the best card counters could compensate for on a one-to-one basis.

Peter Griffin, *Extra Stuff: Gambling Ramblings*

This message has filtered into some of the better casinos in Britain, some years after many of the top Las Vegas casinos learnt it. A casino cannot make any money dealing to empty tables. It can make money either by a narrow percentage on a high turnover, or by a very large percentage on a lower turnover. Many of the high-rolling casinos around Mayfair generally seem to aim for the latter. They offer fairly poor playing conditions and hope to attract mug punters with large bankrolls. By contrast, certain other casinos – the Victoria off the Edgware Road springs to mind – offer better playing conditions, aimed at attracting serious gamblers as well as mug punters. These casinos are generally much fuller and make more money by virtue of their greater turnover, even though their percentage profit at any table may be slightly lower.

Arnold Snyder made the point perfectly:

If card counters actually stopped playing blackjack, the game would die ... The American public *believes* blackjack can be beaten, unaware of the effects of new procedures. Many unscrupulous systems sellers will undoubtedly continue to hype their wares, as always, without mentioning games which are not beatable. The casinos will continue to moan about their losses to counters, as if every other person at their tables were getting rich. But you can't fool all the people all of the time. If the skill factor is permanently removed, the game will die, and the casinos will suffer the most. I do not believe that the casino industry will let this happen.

Blackbelt in Blackjack

I am sure that Arnold Snyder's analysis is correct. As the gambling public becomes more educated, they will simply stay away from games offered by antediluvian casinos that simply want to remove them from as much money as possible, as quickly as possible. By contrast, casinos that offer a better game to all players and welcome the occasional winner tend to be fuller, do more business and make more money. And good luck to them. At least they offer the punter a fair shake for his or her money. At the time of writing, I would single out the Victoria, the Cromwell Mint, and the Gloucester as three casinos in London that offer the punter a reasonable deal.

So I end on a note of qualified optimism. It is possible to win modest amounts in some British casinos, where the skilful player can play on close to equal terms with the house. But do not get too greedy, and do not make the fact that you know what you're doing too obvious. Even the best casinos will not hesitate to bar players they perceive as a threat. To be allowed to go on playing blackjack, you have to: bet scientifically yet appear to be gambling at random; play according to the laws of probability, but seem to be relying on hunches; and above all, convince the casinos that you are a loser.

OTHER GAMES

Can Baccarat be Beaten?

By the late 1980s, my opportunities for playing blackjack were becoming more and more limited. I had been barred from entering most London casinos. In those where I was still able to play, the conditions were such that even the best players would be able to enjoy at best a tiny edge in the game, and I was concerned that if I employed the bet spread necessary to gain an edge, I would be barred from entry.

Given that blackjack was proving increasingly difficult to beat as a practical proposition, I wondered whether there might be other games that would offer a superior opportunity. Baccarat, which is similar in many ways to blackjack, seemed the obvious choice.

Baccarat, known as punto banco in Britain, was first played in medieval Italy. Its name derives from the Italian word *baccara*, meaning zero, the value assigned to all the 10s and court cards in the game.

In Britain, the game is played with six packs of cards which are shuffled by the croupiers and placed into a dealing shoe. Gamblers may bet on either the bank's hand (banco) or the player's hand (punto). Punto and banco are dealt two or three cards each, according to a set of predetermined rules, and the winner is the side with a combined card total nearest to 9. Tens and court cards count as zero; an ace is counted as one; and the other cards have their face value. All cards are summed together, and in all totals of 10 and above the 10 is cancelled. Thus:

$$king + queen = 0$$
$$2 + 9 = 1$$
$$jack + 10 + 4 = 4$$
$$6 + 7 = 3$$
$$9 + 5 = 4$$
$$10 + 9 = 9$$

The final combination, of 10 + 9 for a two-card total of 9, is termed a natural, since it constitutes a hand that wins outright. It is equivalent to a two-card total of 21 in blackjack as an automatic winner. It beats all other hands except other two-card 9s, with which it ties. For a fuller explanation of the rules of baccarat, see Appendix III.

The game is generically close to blackjack. In baccarat, as in blackjack, there are two adversaries and the winner is the one who draws cards nearer a specified total. In both games, the player draws first. In baccarat, however, the player cannot bust.

A further difference between the games is that the gambler in baccarat can bet on either punto or banco, whereas in blackjack the gambler can only bet against the banker. In blackjack, the casino earns its return by virtue of the fact that the dealer draws last and wins all bust player hands. In baccarat, the casino gains its percentage by paying less than even money on banco wins; the pay-off on a winning banco bet is 0.95 units for every 1 unit bet (or 19–20). Punto bets are paid at even money, as for player bets in blackjack.

It seemed to me when I first considered baccarat that the ability to back either punto or banco could give the gambler a significant advantage. I had often reflected on how much easier it would be to make money at blackjack if one was permitted to wager on the dealer's hand. Unfortunately, this idea has also occurred to the casinos.

Baccarat proceeds much more slowly than blackjack. In British punto banco, the game is dealt from a six-deck shoe which typically takes approximately 30 minutes to deal out. This compares with an average time of less than 10 minutes to deal out a four-deck blackjack shoe. The main reason for the slow pace of the game is the time taken to place bets and to pay off winning bets, especially the banco bet with its cumbersome 19–20 return.

A crucial difference between baccarat and blackjack rests in the attitude of the casino. Ever since Dr Thorp published *Beat the Dealer*, the casinos have been aware that blackjack can be beaten, and they are constantly watching out for card counters who place large bets when the shoe is in their favour, whereas Dr Thorp's work on baccarat has lulled the casinos into believing that baccarat cannot be beaten.

In his discussion of baccarat in *The Mathematics of Gambling*, Dr Thorp writes

As the true count varies, the change in player advantage or disadvantage shifts nine times as fast in blackjack as it does in baccarat ... The conclusion is that you might expect to break even or better in eight-deck baccarat about twice as often as you would expect to have an 8 per cent edge in eight-deck blackjack ... The obvious conclusion is that advantages in baccarat are very small, they are very rare, and the few that occur are nearly always in the last 5 to 20 cards in the pack.

Peter Griffin comes to similar conclusions, in *The Theory of Blackjack*:

Betting on 'Bank' or 'Player' whenever the ultimate count suggests an advantage, and not wagering otherwise, would yield a profit of 0.07 per cent of the maximum bet per shoe in Atlantic City (virtually nothing in Las Vegas). Assuming you'll wager $1,000 whenever you get the go ahead, this translates into an expected earning of 70 cents per shoe. In an eight hour day, you might make three bets.

In other words, the effort is a waste of time for the gambler. Because casinos know this, there are no restrictions on the betting spread that a gambler can apply. Indeed, the gambler does not have to bet at all for most of the shoe, and can jump in at any time, with virtually any amount of money up to the table maximum, without arousing suspicion.

Thorp and Griffin's conclusions, however, were based on the assumption of an eight-deck shoe, that might take over an hour to deal out. Playing this game would be a long, unprofitable grind. The British game dealt from a six-deck shoe might offer more frequent opportunities. Furthermore, a much larger average bet size is typical in baccarat than in blackjack. Baccarat has always been a game of the upper classes. A high-rolling blackjack bettor is invariably the focus of casino attention whereas a high-rolling baccarat bettor is following in a long tradition of ruined aristocrats. Baccarat is the high-stakes games par excellence.

There is one final casino condition that applies to baccarat and not to blackjack: the dealer deals out virtually every card from the baccarat shoe. In my first game of baccarat, I noted that the cut card was inserted eight cards from the bottom of the six-deck shoe. In blackjack, it would be rare to find a cut card inserted any lower than a deck from the end of a four-deck shoe.

However, Thorp and Griffin demonstrated that the removal of any card had only about a tenth of the effect on relative advantage in baccarat as in blackjack, so the gambler was far less likely to compensate for losing bets off the top of the shoe with larger winning bets near the bottom.

These considerations gave me cause for concern. It seemed a little unlikely that I alone had discovered the secret of winning baccarat. If two such brilliant individuals as Professors Edward Thorp and Peter Griffin had concluded that baccarat could not be beaten, this was very strong prima facie evidence that baccarat could indeed not be beaten. By seeking to beat the game, I would merely be throwing my bankroll away in a disastrous foray against the immutable laws of probability.

Yet there was one legendary figure in the history of gambling who gave me hope. This was Nico Zographos, the head of the famous Greek syndicate which operated on the French Riviera from the 1920s until the 1950s, taking on all-comers in a baccarat game without limits. By all accounts, Zographos was one of the greatest card players of the twentieth century. He was reputed to be capable of remembering every card that was dealt from a baccarat shoe of 312 cards, of assessing his exact chances of drawing the card he wanted, and of adjusting his playing strategy accordingly. In addition to his phenomenal card memory and his ability to calculate at the speed of a computer, Zographos had nerve and – the most critical ingredient of a truly great player – intuition, that sixth sense that tells a card player when the play is running with the mathematical odds, and when a greater degree of prudence is called for.

Such characteristics could have enabled Zographos to be a formidable player of bridge, blackjack or poker. Instead, he built his fortune at baccarat. His success would seem to bely the conclusions of modern mathematicians. Zographos himself maintained that there is as big a difference between a good baccarat player and a poor one as there is between a scratch golfer and a handicap player. In *Easy Money* David Spanier quotes Zographos as saying:

There is no such thing as luck is all mathematics. There are three kinds of cards – good cards, bad cards and indifferent cards. You must play them according to what they are. That is not a contradiction. You may have luck for an hour or two, even a day or two, even a week. But what people call luck is merely an established fact seen through the spectacles of after events ... The main difference is that the punters usually double when they are losing and hedge when they are winning. I will put it another way: the bank plays baccarat as though it were contract bridge; the punters play baccarat as though it were poker.

Zographos put together a baccarat syndicate willing to accept challenges from all-comers during the inter-war years. A syndicate in gambling, as in business, comprises a group of individuals who pool their skills for their mutual benefit in the belief that the whole is worth more than the sum of its parts.

There were three key members of the Greek syndicate led by Nico Zographos. Zographos himself provided the playing skills. A wealthy Greek shipowner by the name of Vagliano provided the risk capital. A Frenchman, Francois André, who managed casinos at Deauville and Ostend, supplied the business premises.

The syndicate rented space at André's casinos on the basis of paying a 5 per cent commission on all banco's winnings. This was the origin of the casino practice of paying off all winning banco bets at odds of 95–100. The casino did not participate directly in the game because the syndicate's motto was *tout va* – anything goes – that is, the game had no limits. The casino wisely decided not to risk unlimited losses.

The game offered by the Greek syndicate was not the same as that offered in contemporary casinos. It was a variant called 'baccarat en banque', in which the syndicate itself acted as the permanent bank, and dealt out two player (punto) hands. The table had two halves, each of which could accommodate six seated players, and one player hand was dealt to each half of the table. The first two cards dealt to each of the players and the bank were not shown unless either side had a natural 8 or 9, in which case the cards were turned up to claim outright victory. Both the players and the bank had complete discretion on whether to draw a third card or not. The third card was dealt face-up.

The bank's decision on whether or not to draw was therefore based on the value of its first two cards, together with a knowledge of punto's third card dealt face-up when the player elected to draw. Because both punto and banco had complete discretion on whether or not to draw, the game possessed an element of skill that is missing in the contemporary casino game.

The fundamental mathematics of the game were not significantly different from modern punto banco or Nevada baccarat. Given the findings of Professors Thorp and Griffin, one would assume that the skill of the banker would have little long-run effect on the final outcome, although he might be able to extract some advantage from 'reading' the players and inferring whether they had strong or weak hands. However, the evidence is that the banker – in the form of Nico Zographos – did gain a significant advantage through skill.

In more than thirty years, the syndicate only came close to extinction once, at Cannes in 1928. Running a bank of 30 million francs, Zographos as dealer was down to his last million which was riding on a single deal. Zographos dealt the cards, and both players indicated '*Non*', meaning that they were standing with the two cards they had, and implying that they probably held winning hands with totals of between 5 and 7, but neither had a natural 8 or 9 which they would have had to declare. Zographos turned over his own cards, which were a king and queen, with zero value.

Word had gone round that Zographos' credit was exhausted. This was it. As the players and onlookers around the table craned forward, he drew the third card and quietly turned it over. It was a nine, the perfect card. To celebrate the coup, which broke the losing sequence against the syndicate, Zographos bought a nine of diamonds tie-pin with cuff links to match; the nine of diamonds became the pennant on his yacht.

David Spanier, *Easy Money*

From that time on, despite occasional negative fluctuations, the syndicate prospered until Zographos' death in 1953. The extent of his success is attested by the fact that he left an estate worth more than $5 million, which may represent the greatest fortune ever amassed entirely from card playing.

When the syndicate was eventually wiped out, it was with a dealer who played with considerably less skill than Zographos. In August 1957, during the course of several days' play at the Palm Beach Casino in Cannes, an Englishman called Bob Barnett and two Hollywood film producers, Jack Warner and Darryl Zanuck, won some £350,000 playing against the syndicate, a loss from which it never recovered. On the final coup, both players drew a third card – a 2 and 3 respectively. The dealer, holding a two-card total of 5, elected to stand. Drawing a low third card is likely to help the players, since it will add to a low two-card total, so the dealer's decision to stand on 5 was almost certainly wrong. When the cards were turned over, they showed the players holding three-card totals of 6 and 8 respectively, to win. I like to think that, had Zographos still been alive, he would have elected to draw, even though it would have risked Banco's last francs by jeopardizing a total of 5.

Contemporary mathematicians do not claim that baccarat cannot be beaten. They merely claim that the edge that can be obtained is so slight, and arises so infrequently, that it is not worth the effort. As Zographos proved, however, a small edge, if allied with a sound system for money management and a large number of big bets, can generate substantial profits for the dedicated gambler.

Peter Griffin's *Theory of Blackjack* includes an 'ultimate point count' for baccarat which is reproduced in Appendix III. This point count indicates that, as a general principle, high cards of between 5 and 9 help banco while low cards of between 1 (ace) and 4 assist punto.

There are particular card combinations which give either punto or banco a decided edge. In a paper entitled 'Card Counting and Baccarat', David Sklansky demonstrates that in a shoe with three 2s and three 3s left, punto will enjoy a 5–1 advantage over banco; while with a shoe containing only 7s and 8s, banco enjoys a similar edge over punto.

This led Sklansky to speculate whether baccarat could be beaten by counting the cards as they are dealt, in much the same way as blackjack, in order to establish when either punto or banco has an edge. Sklansky's initial conclusion is that it could be, and he suggests a point count weighing 7s and 8s against 2s and 3s. At the end of the paper, however, in a postscript written some time after the original publication, Sklansky concludes:

Since this article was published, Peter Griffin, Edward Thorp and Joel Friedman, among others, have done computer work on baccarat, which shows that the game, while theoretically beatable by counting, is in fact not beatable as a practical matter. This is because profitable bets occur too rarely.

And yet . . . and yet. Hope springs eternal in the gambler's heart, and the critical differences I had noted between baccarat and blackjack might just make the game worth the candle.

I accepted that the effects on each side's advantage are far smaller in blackjack than in baccarat. Even allowing for the fact that the gambler can back either punto or banco, this still means that he or she is almost five times more likely to find good bets in blackjack than in baccarat, other things being equal. But other things are not equal. In particular, the lower depth of the cut card and the greater bet spread possible in baccarat could, according to my hypothesis, more than compensate for this difference.

The first requirement to beat the game was a reliable and usable point-count system. The effect of the removal of any card on relative advantage is not precisely symmetrical between punto and banco but it is close enough for a single point count to suffice for both bets. I devised a card count (described in Appendix III) assigning positive values for the cards between ace and 4 whose removal is good for banco, and negative values to the cards between 5 and 8 whose removal is good for punto. Thus, a high plus count would indicate a surplus of cards between 5 and 8 that would assist banco; a high negative count would indicate a surplus of cards between ace and 4 that would assist punto.

As the cards were dealt out, I would keep a running count, which would be converted to a true count by dividing by the number of decks still to be dealt, just as in blackjack. Thus, a running count of $+10$ after a deck had been dealt (5 decks remaining) would convert to a true count of $+\frac{10}{5} = +2$.

The next step was to calculate when it was worth betting. Overall, I guessed that at true counts between -15 and $+15$, both bets would have a negative expectation. With a true count greater than $+15$, the relative surfeit of high cards would favour banco; while with true counts less than -15 the relative surfeit of low cards would favour punto. This was a working hypothesis from which to start. It was unlikely that any bet would be placed in the first half of the shoe, since this would require a running count in excess of $+60$ or less than -60. But patience would gain its reward in the second half of the shoe as extreme counts became more likely.

My initial bet unit would be £50, rising to £150 on hands where I judged the odds significantly favoured punto or banco. In order not to ruin my carefully cultivated blackjack counting system, which had taken many months to master, I resolved not to try to keep a running count of the baccarat shoe in my head, but rather to note it down on the card generously provided by the casino for the game. This card was provided for punters wishing to record punto or banco wins in their doomed efforts to identify streaks on which they could bet. My running count of the cards dealt therefore aroused no suspicion among the casino personnel.

With modern video surveillance equipment, it would be very easy for the security room to zoom in on a player and analyse exactly what he or she is writing down on a card. To be absolutely certain of avoiding the possibility of detection, the baccarat player would have to keep the running count in his head rather than on paper, and also make accurate true count conversions mentally.

The results of my system to date are inconclusive. I have won just over £2,000 but have bet on less than a thousand hands, which is not a statistically significant sample. My positive result could simply represent a standard deviation from an expected negative outcome, which would prevail as play was extended further.

The limited sample makes me suspect that it *may* be possible to gain a modest edge by betting either on punto or banco in the last two decks of a six-deck shoe, and particularly in the last deck. I express this view tentatively, for two main reasons.

First, the application of the system in practice is tedious to the point of boredom. It requires sitting at a punto banco table and counting, but not betting at all, down the first three or four decks dealt out. It can take up to half an hour before the dealer reaches the final two decks of cards, where things might start to get interesting. The mediocre coffee and sandwiches supplied by the casinos are hardly adequate compensation for these long waiting periods.

Second, the process would be less boring if it were a prelude to betting significant amounts of money – say £1,000 a hand. But to put this sort of money into action with an estimated 1 per cent advantage would require a bankroll of £100,000. In addition, if a baccarat bettor started placing these sorts of sums into action and winning, casino personnel would start paying very close attention indeed. If they suspected that the bettor's edge was achieved by card counting, they would immediately take counter-measures. In 1990s London, Nico Zographos, far from being respected for his skills at the card table, would instead be politely shown the door.

Nick the Greek and
the Icarus Syndrome

In 1949, a millionaire gambler by the name of Nick Dandalos arrived in Las Vegas with a proposition that was to lead to one of the most famous gambling contests of all time. He issued an open challenge to the gamblers of Nevada to a poker game without limits which would continue until one of the players gave up or was wiped out.

At that time, Las Vegas was one of the few towns in the USA where such a challenge was legal.

Among the entrepreneurs who had arrived recently was a Texan gambler called Benny Binion. Gambling was still illegal in Texas in 1946, and Benny had to leave the state in a hurry when, in his words, 'my sheriff got beat in the election'. He headed for Las Vegas, where he acquired a nondescript casino formerly known as the El Dorado Club. He changed its name to the Golden Horseshoe and set about improving both its image and its business prospects.

Always on the lookout for some publicity to attract gamblers into his casino, Benny's interest was aroused when Nick 'the Greek' Dandalos hit town.

Poker poses something of a problem for casino owners. On the one hand, it is a popular gambling pastime and they would like to offer it to their prospective clientele. On the other hand, the outcome of the game is not mathematically determined but depends on a mix of mathematics, playing skill and psychology. Consequently it is not easy for casinos to extract a guaranteed percentage from the game. The two most common methods now employed are for the casino to take out a fixed percentage of each pot, and to charge players a fixed amount per hour for sitting down at the poker tables. The first method is akin to the 5 per cent commission paid by the Greek syndicate to the casinos where it dealt baccarat. The second method is employed to finance the poker room of Britain's largest casino, the Victoria Club off the Edgware Road in London, where players are charged a fee upwards of £5 per hour in proportion to the size of the stakes on the table.

Benny Binion used neither method. When he met Nick Dandalos, he offered to set the game up free of charge, provided the game was held in public in his casino. His idea was that a game of this size would attract visitors into the Golden Horseshoe to watch it, and thereby provide better marketing for the club than a million dollars' worth of advertising.

Dandalos agreed to Benny Binion's proposal, and Binion then contacted an old gambling crony of his from Texas, one Johnny Moss. Moss had just completed a four-day playing marathon, but when he heard of Nick the Greek's challenge he drove all the way from Texas to Nevada without a break, shook hands with his opponent, and sat down to play.

The game was to last five months. The players broke every few days to sleep, although Dandalos spent much of his rest time playing craps. Apart from these breaks the game was continuous. It is now generally recognized as the world's first unofficial poker championship. It was essentially a head-to-head showdown between Dandalos and Moss, although other players were permitted to join the game for a $10,000 buy-in. As Benny Binion had hoped, it attracted a large number of fascinated observers, who at times stood six deep around the poker table to watch the protagonists in action. When they weren't watching the game, their business on the other tables in the club swelled the Horseshoe's profits and laid the basis of Benny Binion's fortune.

The game of poker is mathematical in its conception, but at higher levels of play it is psychological in its resolution. The ranking of hands is in inverse relationship to the probability of their occurrence – hands that are mathematically less likely beat hands that are more likely to be dealt. The highest ranking hand of all is a royal flush (ace, king, queen, jack and ten of the same suit) which is the least likely of all hands to be dealt. A player would expect to be dealt this hand less than once in every 650,000 hands.

The ranking of other poker hands is shown in the table below.

Moss and Dandalos began their contest by playing five-card stud. This is the most basic form of poker in which each player is dealt five cards in sequence. After anteing up their initial bet (an ante is the bet placed before the first cards are dealt), the first card was dealt face-down or 'in the hole', while the second card was dealt face-up. There then followed three rounds of betting after which the third, fourth and fifth cards were dealt.

Hand	Description	Probability of being dealt in 5 cards (per cent)
Straight flush	5 cards of the same suit in sequence	0.01
Four of a kind	4 cards of the same value	0.02
Full house	3 of a kind combined with a pair	0.14
Flush	5 cards of the same suit	0.20
Straight	5 cards in sequence	0.39
Three of a kind	3 cards of the same value	2.11
Two pairs	2 pairs combined	4.75
One pair	2 cards of the same value	42.26
High card	Single highest card dealt	50.12

There is no playing skill in this game; the player's only decisions are whether to fold the hand (i.e. concede), to check (i.e. to pass the betting across to the other player), or to continue betting, and if so how much.

In the game played by Moss and Dandalos, the antes were $100 a hand, and the player with the lowest card showing after the first two had been dealt was required to start the betting with a $200 wager.

The successful poker player is one who knows the probabilities of different outcomes and respects those probabilities. In his classic book, *The Education of a Poker Player* (1957), Herbert Osborne Yardley established a series of mathematical rules for deciding whether or not to play out different hands. In the game of seven-card stud, where the players are each initially dealt three cards of which two are hidden and one displayed, Yardley recommended only staying in with three-card hands of three of a kind; a pair of aces, kings or queens; or a three-card draw to a flush or a straight. In Yardley's view, it would only be worth staying in with a low pair of jacks or less if it is supported by an ace or king as the third card. Any other hand should be folded.

Yardley set out a similar series of rules for deciding whether to stay in the pot after a fourth and fifth card have been drawn. For example, he advised not drawing to an inside straight, since the odds against completing the hand are very high. An inside straight is a sequence such as jack-10-9-7, which can be completed only by drawing the 'inside' card of 8. Of the 48 cards not in the player's hands, four (the four 8s) will complete the hand, while 44 will leave the player with at best a pair. The additional card is therefore only worth buying in the unlikely event that there is more than eleven times as much money on the table as the player is required to bet. The amount of money that the player has already put into the pot is irrelevant to the decision as to whether or not to draw.

Similar considerations apply to the decision to draw or fold an outside straight. An outside straight is a hand such as jack-10-9-8 which can be completed by drawing a card to either side of it. This is a far more attractive proposition than an inside straight, since of the 48 cards not in the hand, eight will complete it (any one of the four queens or four 7s) while 40 will not – offering odds against of 40–8 or 5–1. This would represent value for money provided that there was more than five times as much money in the pot as the required bet. If not, the hand should be folded. Similarly, the odds against completing a four-card flush are 39–9 against, or 4.33–1, so the rational player's decision as to whether to draw depends on whether the amount of money in the pot is more than 4.33 times the required bet.

All these odds will be affected by how many of the other players' cards are displayed, and what are their values and suits. A skilful poker player would be able to make the appropriate adjustments virtually instantaneously.

Yardley also applied the laws of probability to determine his recommended betting strategy. With a relatively weak opener such as two queens, he recommended a high bet to drive out as many other players as possible. With a strong opener such as three of a kind, he recommended staying in with the minimum bet required in order to keep as many other players in the pot as possible. His reasoning was that three of a kind is likely to be a winning hand even if every other player plays out the hand, and consequently a player who holds three of a kind will maximize his winnings by feigning weakness to encourage others to stay in the pot. By contrast, an opener of two queens may well be too weak to win a showdown against several other hands drawn to completion.

Yardley's application of the laws of probability may appear trivial to a mathematician. But to many poker players, accustomed to playing by hunch rather than rational calculation, they came as a revelation. Yardley estimated that a player who applied his rules would play one in seven of all hands dealt, win 40 per cent of the hands for which he played and lose the remaining 60 per cent. He calculated that a player who followed these rules should grind ahead over a long series of trials – provided that the antes were nominal. If the antes were high, then a player playing according to Yardley's conservative rules could be 'anted away', or lose his bankroll by folding mediocre hands while waiting for a potential winner to develop.

It can be assumed that serious poker players have a detailed knowledge of the mathematical odds involved and of the Yardley strategy. Someone playing strictly according to Yardley's rules effectively reveals his cards to the other players. For example, in a game of seven-card stud where the first two cards dealt are hidden and the third card displayed, a Yardley player who buys a fourth card with a 7 showing can only have three 7s; two 7s with an ace or king in support; a three-card straight or flush sequence containing a 7; or a single 7 with a concealed pair of aces or kings.

The most likely alternatives are that the player holds a pair of 7s or a three-card straight or flush sequence containing a 7 (with the odds against him completing it). Given this limited range of possibilities, a player holding two 8s with an ace in support can confidently stay in the pot (contrary to Yardley's rules) knowing that he is probably winning at this stage of the draw. The decisions after the fourth and fifth cards then depend on the cards drawn by each player.

This example demonstrates the general principle that the higher the level of play, the less the relative importance of mathematics and the greater the importance of psychology. Reading the opposition involves a whole range of factors, including assessing your protagonist's system of play – whether he is a 'tight' player like Yardley who stays in the pot on one out of seven deals when holding a strong hand, or a 'loose' player who stays in more frequently with weaker hands in the hope of bluffing out opponents or catching a winning card later in the deal.

The work of world poker champions of the 1970s and 1980s such as Doyle Brunson and Bobby Baldwin reveals that their objective is to keep their opponents guessing. Sometimes they play tightly, sometimes loosely; they constantly change gear without warning. Their objective is never to let the opposition know what they are thinking, and so induce them to guess wrong on key hands, bluffing them out of potential winners by aggressive betting, or sucking them into big pots by feigning weakness on strong hands.

Before one can progress to this level of expertise, it is essential to have complete mastery of the mathematical probabilities of the game. Without chat, psychological ploys are mere castles in the air.

So it proved in the contest between Johnny Moss and Nick the Greek. The most famous hand they played was a hand of five-card stud, which resulted in something between quarter and half a million dollars changing hands.

From the table of probabilities, it can be deduced that a player could usually expect to win a head-to-head game of five-card stud if dealt a single pair. Given the rules of the game, the biggest bets would also be likely on such hands. A player would be unlikely to gamble aggressively on a single high card, since there would be a chance of losing the entire amount on the final draw. Conversely, given that only the first card is concealed in five-card stud, if one player was developing a strong hand of two pairs or better, at least one pair would be showing by the time the fourth card was drawn. Even if a hand that was developing into a straight or flush failed to complete on the final draw, the risk that it might be completed would normally restrain the betting until it was clear that it was busted.

By contrast, where one player holds a pair which has been completed by his hole (concealed) card, he could be tempted to bet aggressively knowing that he was winning at that stage of the draw, and that the more cards drawn, the lower the chances of being outdrawn by the opposition.

This was the reasoning of Johnny Moss. On the hand in question, Moss was dealt a 9 in the hole and 6 exposed; Nick the Greek was showing a 7. Johnny Moss related how the hand developed:

Low man brings it in (bets first). I bet two hunnerd with a 6, he raises fifteen hunnerd or two thousand, I call him. The next card comes, I catch a 9, he catches a 6. I got two 9s then. I make a good bet – five thousand maybe – an' he plays back at me, twenty-five thousand. I jus' call him. I'm figurin' to take all that money of his, an' I don't want to scare him none. The next card comes. He catches a trey, I catch a deuce. Ain't nuttin' he got can beat my two 9s.

Alvarez, *The Biggest Game in Town*

At this point Moss had a pair of 9s (one concealed), a 6 and a 2. Nick the Greek was showing a 7, 6 and 3, with one card hidden. Whatever the concealed card, Moss knew that with four cards drawn, he was winning. The Greek's best possible hand was a pair of 7s. Alternatively, he could have a 4 concealed, and so be drawing to a possible straight if he pulled a 5 on his final card – but with seven cards known, the odds against that were 11–1. Moss placed the Greek on a pair, probably of 7s. If that was the case, Moss could only be beaten if the Greek completed three of a kind with his final draw; and the odds against that were 21–1. Any way Moss calculated it, he was winning, and he wanted to maximize his win.

I check then to trap him, an' he bets, jus' like I wanted. So I raise him wa-ay up there, an' he calls. I got him in there, all right. There's a hunnerd thousand dollars in that pot – maybe more, I don't know exactly – an' I'm a-winnin' it. On the end (final card dealt), I catch a trey, he catches a jack. He's high now with the jack an' he bets fifty thousand. I can't put him on jack in the hole, you know. He ain't gonna pay all the way jus' for the chance to outdraw me. I don't care what he catches, he's gotta beat those two 9s of mine. So I move in with the rest of my money.

The way Moss calculated, he had to have the hand won. The only way he could lose was if Nick the Greek had been dealt a jack as his first (concealed) card, and then drawn a winning pair of jacks on the fifth card. But Moss discounted this possibility on the grounds that the Greek would not have bet so aggressively holding only a single jack, since he had to assume that Moss held a pair.

At this point, Nick the Greek looked at Johnny Moss, and said softly, 'Mr Moss, I think I have a jack in the hole.'

Moss was incredulous. 'Greek, if you've got a jack down there, you're liable to win yourself one hell of a pot.'

After a long silence, Nick the Greek pushed his own chips forward to call Johnny Moss, and turned over his hole card. It was the jack of diamonds.

'He outdrew me,' commented Moss philosophically. 'We had about two hunnerd an' fifty thousand dollars apiece in that pot, an' he won it. But that's all right. That's better than all right. If he's gonna go chasin' dreams like that, I know I'm gonna break him in the end.'

It took him five months, but eventually Johnny Moss wore down Nick the Greek. At the end, when the Greek lost his last pot, he got up from the table, smiled, and said in a soft voice, 'Mr Moss, I have to let you go.' He then bowed slightly, and went upstairs to bed. It is rumoured that he had lost two million dollars.

The seeds of the Greek's nemesis were sown even as he raked in that pot of half a million dollars with his winning pair of jacks. While Moss had played the hand scientifically, the Greek had played it recklessly. Although he won that particular hand, he won it against the odds. Any gambler can win against the odds in the short term if luck is on his side. But the longer play goes on, the more likely it is that he will be ground down to defeat.

Even as he watched the biggest single pot of their contest disappear,

Johnny Moss knew that if the Greek went on playing as he had on that hand, 'chasin' dreams', he would eventually lose his money. He also guessed that the fact that Dandalos had won that hand might encourage him to play even more recklessly in the future.

Johnny Moss went on to become the world's first official poker champion in 1970, when Benny Binion formalized the contest in his Golden Horseshoe Casino. He won it again in 1971 and 1974:

In those days, it warn't no one game an' it warn't no freeze-out. You had to win all the games, win all the money. Then you're the best player, an' they vote on you. A lot of gamblers hate me, but they still vote on me being the best player in the world. It was pretty nice, you know, because there were a lot of good players in town. But most good players are only good at one game, an' I'm good at 'em all. I win all five games in 1970.

In *Big Deal*, his entertaining account of a year on the professional poker circuit, Anthony Holden related how he came upon Benny Binion and Johnny Moss in a Las Vegas restaurant one evening in May 1989, about nine months before Benny Binion died.

I was just thinking of the Great Game with the Greek all those years ago, and of how much subsequent poker history was now sat in that corner, when Moss gestured me over to join them. 'What you doin' here, son? You shoulda stuck to your run down there.' Without listening to whatever explanation I muttered, he went on, 'Have a drink. We're celebrating. D'you know what we're celebrating?' All I knew was that his birthday fell in May, near mine. 'No, no,' he said, 'and it ain't Easter either.' He looked at Binion, who cracked a grin. 'Benny and I are celebrating seventy-five years of friendship.'

Benny Binion was to die nine months later, but at the time it seemed he was immortal. I raised my glass in an awestruck toast, listened to a few of their childhood tales, and then felt I should leave them to it. I know when I am out of my league.

In contrast to this happy ending, Nick the Greek died penniless on Christmas Day 1966. His early luck deserted him after his showdown with Johnny Moss, and his winning hand of two jacks proved to be the zenith of his career.

Although his fortune was gradually dissipated on the gaming tables of Las Vegas, Dandalos never lost his reputation as a gentleman. He never indulged in self-pity, even though he must have been fully aware of the enormity of his fall from the time when he had challenged anyone in the world to a poker game without limits. On one occasion not long before his death, when he was reduced to playing five- and ten-dollar draw in the poker rooms of Gardena, California, someone suggested sarcastically that he had come down a bit in the world. He merely replied in his soft voice, 'It's action, isn't it?'

For me, Dandalos resembles a Shakespearean hero, imbued with many virtues – courage, dignity and humility – yet ultimately brought to grief by one fatal flaw. That flaw was that he desired action above all else. He summed up his philosophy when he said, 'The next best thing to gambling and winning is gambling and losing.'

Here was a man who, like Icarus, challenged the gods. For a brief time he soared above other mortals. Yet he flew in the face of the laws of probability, and his final fate had a tragic inevitability about it. His luck melted away like the wings of Icarus and he plunged to destruction.

Such is the destiny of all those compelled by some psychological quirk to gamble when the odds are against them.

Epilogue

Beyond the Green Baize Tables

It is remarkable that a science which began with the consideration of games of chance should have become the most important object of human knowledge ... The most important questions of life are, for the most part, really only problems of probability.

Pierre Simon, Marquis de Laplace, *Theorie Analytique des Probabilities*, 1812

Since the time of Blaise Pascal, the real motivation of many of those who have studied gambling problems has been to apply their general principles to the real world. In the controlled, mathematical world of the casino, the choices available are limited and success or failure is measured only in gambling chips. In the world outside, the range of choices is wider, the conditions less controlled, and the measures of success more diverse. Yet the principles for successful decision-making are the same.

Perhaps the links between the casino and the outside world are most evident in the spheres of finance and investment. It is no coincidence that many successful casino gamblers moved on to make their fortunes on the world's stock markets. Edward Thorp, the father of modern card counting, built his fortune by exploiting pricing inefficiencies on Wall Street. Applying the same mathematical techniques he had used to gain an edge at the blackjack tables, he identified situations in which warrants that provide an option to buy a company's stock were mispriced relative to the underlying stock, thus providing an opportunity for arbitrage.

Arbitrage involves holding two conflicting positions in the same company – for example, buying an underpriced warrant while selling the overpriced shares – so that a profit is guaranteed no matter which way the share price moves. If the share price falls, the arbitrageur buys back the shares he has sold to close his position at a profit greater than the cost of the warrants. Conversely, if the share price rises, the price of the warrants associated with them rises more than proportionately, and again the arbitrageur closes his position at a profit.

A successful gambler – one who is able, apart from occasional negative fluctuations, to make a consistent profit from gambling – is essentially an arbitrageur who earns a percentage from gambling by exploiting market inefficiencies. This is most obvious in the case of gamblers who visit racetracks and move from one bookmaker to another, seeking to take advantage of variations in the odds offered by different bookmakers. The objective is to back all the horses in a given race at the best odds offered by different bookies, so that the pay-off secured on each horse exceeds the combined value of the bets placed, and the gambler will earn a positive return from the race whichever horse wins.

With advances in communications technology and successive increases in the taxation charge levied by government, arbitrage opportunities have become much more difficult to find. Contemporary gamblers and investors rarely have the guaranteed profit offered by arbitrage, but must seek out 'value for money' in their operations. Value-for-money bets, where the expected pay-off is greater than the price on offer, do not have the same one-way profit potential offered by arbitraging; but if the speculator has positioned himself or herself correctly, such bets should generate positive returns over a long series of trials.

Successful speculators and successful gamblers personify Gramsci's aphorism, that the road to success lies through 'pessimism of the intelligence; optimism of the will'.

Pessimism of the intelligence requires a careful, prudent assessment of the risks and returns associated with any position. If the prospective returns do not appear to justify the risks involved, a speculator will simply stay out of the market. Success requires the patience to go on waiting as long as it takes for the odds to swing decisively in your favour.

Optimism of the will requires that, once you are sure the odds are in your favour, you stick to your assessment no matter what the crowd is doing. By definition, for the odds to be favourable to the gambler, most of the money must be betting in the wrong direction. It requires nerve to go against the crowd by supporting that judgement with hard cash. Successful gamblers, like successful financiers, are often loners, prepared to take advice and glean information from many sources, but ultimately ready to make up their own minds. As the master investor

Benjamin Graham observed, 'The fact that other people agree or disagree with you makes you neither right nor wrong. You will be right if your facts and reasoning are correct.'

This is demonstrated by the man who is probably the most successful living professional investor, Warren Buffett. Buffett has risen from modest beginnings to become one of the three wealthiest men in the USA. His Berkshire Hathaway investment company enjoyed a compound annual return of approximately 24 per cent in the 27 years between 1965 and 1992. This means that a dollar invested in Berkshire Hathaway in 1965 would have grown to $338 by 1992 – an impressive performance by any standards. It compares to an average return of 11 per cent per annum that would have been earned from an index of stock market investments. A comparison of these two figures suggests that Buffett is to the average investor what an Olympic 100-metre sprint champion is to a Sunday afternoon jogger.

It might be thought that Buffett has achieved these results through a combination of luck and aggressive speculation – the same methods applied by the Prince of Canino to win a fortune at the roulette tables of the Homburg Kursaal over a century ago. In fact, nothing could be further from the truth. Buffett's two guiding rules are:

Rule Number One: Never lose money.
Rule Number Two: Never forget Rule Number One.

The principles on which he has built his fortune are the same as those which any successful gambler must adopt. They may be summed up in eight statements.

1 *Keep your speculative capital separate from money which you need to live, and never borrow to speculate.*

Buffett has never borrowed to invest. His approach is like that of professional gambler Lawrence Revere, who advised that a gambler should 'always play within his bankroll, using no more than a percentage of it as a playing stake. Betting scared money is bad gambling.' (*Playing Blackjack as a Business*).

The legendary Johnny Moss, arguably the greatest poker player of the twentieth century, had a foolproof method for keeping his gambling capital separate from his other resources so that he would never be tempted to bet more than he could afford to lose. He handed a slice of his winnings to his wife and never borrowed from her when he lost. In an interview with Jon Bradshaw, quoted in *Fast Company*, Moss commented wrily:

I never touch our house money. I'd rather borrow from a bellhop than ask my wife for a penny. Me and my wife was born poor, we had good times and bad and we been married near to fifty years. Now I may be broke, or as near to broke as can be, but Virgie, my wife, well, Virgie's a millionaire.

2   *Money is not important in itself. It is merely a measure of the success of the strategy being pursued.*

Like many of the world's top gamblers, Buffett has a radically different attitude towards money from the average man. He does not view it as a commodity to be expended in pursuit of material affluence, but rather as a mark of success to be accumulated for its own sake. Despite his status as a multi-billionaire, Buffett lives comfortably but not extravagantly in the cattle town of Omaha, Nebraska, where he was brought up.

Professional gamblers have a similar attitude. The name of the game is to win for its own sake, not to spend conspicuously. In *Big Deal*, Anthony Holden notes that what distinguishes the world's leading professional poker players from the rest is their attitude towards money.

If I had learnt one truth all year, it was that poker's ultimate players are distinguished by one remarkable quality: a serene indifference to the worldly attributes of money. To most of us, money is a method of keeping score, not merely in poker, but in life. To these guys, money is their daily bread only in the sense that it is part of their professional equipment.

This is confirmed by Johnny Moss. In Jon Bradshaw's *Fast Company* he is quoted as saying, 'I don't have much regard for money. Money's just paper to gamble with and when I leave the table I don't pay it no mind.'

3   *A winning strategy requires you to identify situations where prices do not reflect true values.*

Successful investors, like successful gamblers, are constantly looking for situations where prices are out of line with true values. Since most people are not mugs, such situations do not arise frequently. They need to be sought out with thorough and continuous research. Their identification requires the application of a scientific methodology to determine true value and compare it with the price on offer.

Warren Buffett will spend many months trawling through company reports, interviewing company managements and reflecting on the markets in which his companies operate, before taking an investment position. He will apply a range of objective criteria including asset values, dividend yields and market position to determine a company's true value, and he will buy into it only when its price is significantly lower than that value.

Similarly, all the successful gamblers described in this book – such as Darnborough and Jaggers on the roulette wheel, or Revere and Uston at the blackjack table – had clear criteria for determining value bets where the true probability of success exceeded the odds being offered.

4   *In order to beat the market or the casino, you need to know far more than other players.*

There is a continuous stream of new ideas and theories about finance and gambling. Some of the most valuable are buried deep in obscure technical journals. The player who can get hold of them, and realize their practical money-making potential, has an enormous advantage over others.

Ordinary gamblers and speculators are frequently characterized by a belief that they can win through simply by feel or hunch without undertaking a great deal of painstaking research. The top players, whether in the stock market or the casino, never stop researching.

5   *There is no such thing as easy money. Anyone who tells you differently is either a fool, a charlatan, or both.*

In his book on Warren Buffett, John Train says:

Without doubt one of the biggest differences between the ones that make it and the ones that don't is simply that the successful ones have the drive to win through in spite of all the frustrations. The difference between the professional and the amateur is often just that the professional will work terribly hard and keep at it. It takes so much concentration to be in the top rank that, although great investors are almost always rich, they rarely live in a grandiose way during their most successful period.

The Midas Touch

The only way to make money consistently, whether in the casino or on the stock market, is by grinding away, day after day, month after month, seeking situations where the price on offer is lower than the value being purchased. If value for money does not exist, no system of money management has ever been devised that could turn a negative expectation into a positive result. In the words of the nineteenth-century roulette player George Augustus Sala, attempts to beat the game by money management techniques alone are merely 'imbecile systems evolved from the distempered brains of gamblers'.

6 *When you do find outstanding value, bet aggressively within the limits of your bankroll.*

Once Warren Buffett identifies a position he believes to be of outstanding value in relation to price, he will commit a large part of his bankroll to it. Philip Fisher once said, 'I don't want a lot of good investments; I want a few outstanding ones.' Buffett also follows this tenet. The *Financial Times* of 23 June 1991 reported that 85 per cent of Buffett's investments were in just four companies. My own view is that such a narrow spread of risk would carry an unacceptably high chance of ruin should anything go wrong. But then again, Buffett does not need my approval – his results speak for themselves.

Successful gamblers are likely to seek a wider spread of bets to minimize their risk of ruin, but they also bet aggressively in favourable situations. Ken Uston's blackjack teams operated on this principle – they won by betting heavily when the cards were in their favour. Poker players do the same. Reading *Big Deal*, it appears that Anthony Holden's entire profit of $12,000 earned from a year of playing poker came from no more than half-a-dozen hands.

7 *If your position does not yield immediate profits, stick to it provided you are confident of the soundness of the underlying strategy. In the long run, prices will come back into line with values.*

This requires strength of character. Every gambler and investor can expect long stretches when they are sitting on a losing position. Negative fluctuations from the expected result will be as common as positive fluctuations. Sitting them out can be a lonely and depressing business, as Ken Uston recalls in *Million Dollar Blackjack*:

Several years ago, I played blackjack for 22 consecutive days in the most favourable games I've ever experienced. At the end of 22 days, I was down $35,000. On the 23rd day I lost again. After the session, I disgustedly returned to the team meeting room and announced, 'I've had it. You guys keep playing. I'm going back to San Francisco. If I see one more stiff, I'll tear the cards up.' One of the guys said, 'You're just tired, Ken. Get a good night's sleep. You'll get 'em eventually.'

My point: here I'd been playing full time for over two years and should have been aware of the steepness of the negative swings. Yet I was almost ready to throw in the towel. (The cards did turn; the very next day, I beat the Trop out for $12,000, the start of a $97,000 winning streak.)

Similarly, patience is one of the cornerstones of Warren Buffett's investment philosophy. He adopts a buy-and-hold strategy for stocks he considers offer value for money. In his 1991 Berkshire Hathaway Annual Report, Buffett commented chat 'Our stay-put behaviour reflects our view chat the stockmarket serves as a relocation centre at which money is moved from the active to the patient.'

8 *If you do succeed, cash in your chips and take a break.*
Buffett periodically liquidates his portfolio when he feels conditions are no longer favourable, as any good gambler should. He cashed in his investments in 1969, when he felt he could get a better return on the interest earned on cash deposits. Four years later, in 1973/74, the world's stock markets experienced their worst declines since the Great Crash of 1929. Feeling that stock market prices were now below true values, Buffett started buying again, and by mid-1979 he was urging his investors, 'If one is ever going to buy common stocks, the time to buy them is now. It screams at you.' The boom of the 1980s followed, and Buffett duly cashed out again in 1986 when he felt that prices had run ahead of true values. He missed the top of the boom as a result – but he also missed the crash of October 1987.

One of the marks of a successful gambler is knowing when to quit. The baccarat player Nico Zographos owed his success in no small measure to knowing when to say, '*C'est assez pour ce soir*' ('that's enough for tonight'). Win or lose, he knew that he could not maintain peak performance indefinitely, and that playing too long would be fatal to his chances of success.

The principles chat determine success in gambling and finance also apply to politics. They may be illustrated by examining the rise and fall of Margaret Thatcher.

Of all the assessments of her remarkable career, one of the shrewdest was tucked away in an obscure journal called the *Investors' Chronicle*. In its edition of 5 July 1991, it contained an article by Matthew Parris, who had observed the Thatcher Government at first hand as a Conservative Member of Parliament during the mid-1980s.

In the politics of the last 15 years, Mrs Thatcher has been more than a personality: she has been a sort of primal force ... All the commentators emphasize her force – and they are right, for there has been nobody of equal force at Westminster since Churchill. Almost all go on to praise her courage and her intellect. Here they are mistaken. Judged against her political peers, Mrs

Thatcher was not unusually intelligent nor particularly brave ... Her 'courage' was not courage, but nerve, for never in her political career was Mrs Thatcher brave in any important cause she did not think she could win. Examples of her surrender in the face of superior strength punctuate her career. Rhodesia, the NHS, education vouchers, the ERM ...

But if she thought a line could be held, then she held it. *She would reach a cool gambler's judgement on the odds and, having reached it, her nerve never let her intellect down.* When she threw her hat into the ring against Heath it took nerve but it was rational; she had nothing to lose. When she despatched the task force to the South Atlantic she balanced the risk of defeat with the certainty, had Britain capitulated, of her own political demise. She backed down to Scargill when his strength was high and took him on when she knew she could win.

'A Leader of Enduring Qualities' (my italics)

According to Parris, Margaret Thatcher was essentially a successful gambler who was only prepared to commit herself to a particular position when the odds were in its favour.

This is not a commonly accepted judgement. In contrast to, say, Harold Wilson, the Labour Prime Minister during the 1960s and 1970s whose every move seemed to be based on a tactical assessment of risk and return with little strategic vision, Margaret Thatcher is generally held up as an example of a 'conviction politician' who never compromised her principles. Nevertheless, I believe that historians will vindicate the judgement of Matthew Parris.

Parris does not analyse the reasons for Mrs. Thatcher's abrupt fall in November, 1990, but his analysis of her as a gambler may provide some clues.

By the late 1980s, Mrs. Thatcher had led her party to victory in three successive general elections and been in office for ten years. She seemed to be in complete command of her party, parliament and the world stage. She was like a gambler on a roll. But for a gambler there is no time more dangerous than when everything is going according to plan. In such circumstances it is too easy for a gambler's cool judgement to erode and for complacency to creep in. When it seems that the gambler can hardly lose, the bets get higher and higher, and the risk of ruin, if anything should go wrong, correspondingly increases.

So it was with Margaret Thatcher. Little by little, after so much success, complacency gave way to arrogance. Instead of coolly assessing the risks and returns associated with any course of action, she began to allow her emotions to override her reason. She ignored the concern of her supporters over issues such as the Poll Tax and Britain's role in Europe. She began to treat some of her colleagues in government with something approaching contempt. When the Deputy Prime Minister resigned rather than face continual humiliation, her most dangerous opponent within the party, Michael Heseltine, emerged from the wings. Far from heading off the danger by meeting the opposition half-way, she appeared to goad Heseltine into running against her for the leadership by suggesting that he did not have the nerve to do so. This in turn more or less forced Heseltine's hand – had he not run against her, he would have been accused of cowardice and his own career would have been finished.

A professional gambler would have advised Margaret Thatcher that there was no percentage in forcing an opponent's hand in this way. As it was, she failed to win a decisive majority on the first ballot of the ensuing leadership election, and was forced to resign.

The rise and fall of Margaret Thatcher followed the elliptical path of a gambler who first plays according to the probabilities, but whose judgement is then corroded by success and who ultimately plunges to destruction.

In politics there are few absolutes. Whatever the short-term fluctuations, long-term success depends, not on courage or justice or truth, but rather on an accurate assessment of the odds.

The same is true in other spheres of life. For professional gamblers, correct assessment of probabilities is the only thing that stands between them and penury. In order to identify favourable situations, they must be prepared to go against popular opinion. It is no coincidence that the small band of professional gamblers are all, to some degree, outsiders and misfits. They live on the margins of society, rejecting the conventions of a nine-to-five existence and reluctant to accept authority.

There is a curious paradox in this. Professional gamblers must possess immense self-discipline in order to succeed, yet they are unwilling to have discipline imposed upon them and are generally suspicious of those in authority. A mistrust of authority may be the common factor leading gamblers to their chosen career. Most of them could make more money, and certainly easier money, pursuing a more orthodox profession, because the qualities necessary for success in gambling are also needed for more socially acceptable pursuits such as business, politics and finance.

Natural ability is a necessary but not sufficient condition for success. It must be allied with prudent judgement, often exercised under conditions of intense pressure on the basis of incomplete data and under tight time constraints. This requires a high degree of emotional control. Moreover, many decisions, even in theoretically favourable conditions, will have negative results. So a further vital quality for success is perseverance. Above all, it is necessary to avoid the temptation of seeking to win back a losing position with one dramatic coup which, if it comes off, will yield impressive returns, but if it fails will spell ruin. Success in gambling is achieved only through a long, hard grind through negative fluctuations.

Success can also spell danger if it breeds complacency. Perhaps the most critical requirement for consistent achievement is humility. A gambler must never forget, no matter how successful he or she may be in the short term, that over a long period no individual, no matter how gifted, can beat the laws of probability.

To win consistently, a gambler must thus possess a combination of qualities so rare and so virtuous that under other circumstances it might be regarded as heroic.

Professional gamblers are not generally regarded as heroes. The casinos deploy the full power of modern surveillance technology to identify and eliminate any gamblers who are winning money through the application of mathematical methods. The government and the Gaming Board support the casinos' right to bar any gamblers they suspect of having an edge, regarding them as no more than parasites who feed off society while contributing nothing to it. But for my part I salute professional gamblers wherever they may be, and wish them success in their endeavours.

APPENDICES

Appendix I

Mathematical Expectation and Standard Deviation in Roulette

The mathematical expectation of the financial return from any bet is defined by the formula: *Pay-off for each result multiplied by the mathematical probability of each result*. Or, formally,

$$e = (w \times p) - (b \times q)$$

where e = the mathematically expected return
w = pay-off for a winning bet
p = probability of a win
b = value of the bet
q = probability of a loss

In roulette, the mathematically expected return from a bet on an even-money chance may be computed from this formula as follows:

$$(+\tfrac{1}{1} \times \tfrac{18}{37}) \qquad + (-\tfrac{1}{1} \times \tfrac{18}{37}) \qquad + (-\tfrac{1}{1} \times \tfrac{1}{37} \times \tfrac{1}{2})$$
$$\text{return on a win} \quad \text{return on a loss} \quad \text{return on a zero}$$

Thus, if a gambler places a bet of £100 on a red number, there is a chance of $\tfrac{18}{37}$ that the bet will win and be paid off at 1–1; there is a chance of $\tfrac{18}{37}$ that the bet will lose if the ball lands on one of the 18 non-red numbers; and there is a $\tfrac{1}{37}$ chance that the bet will be placed *en prison* if the zero comes up, with a 50 per cent expectation of getting it back on the next spin. In monetary terms, the expected return may be calculated as:

$$(£100 \times \tfrac{18}{37}) + (-£100 \times \tfrac{18}{37}) + (-£100 \times \tfrac{1}{37} \times \tfrac{1}{2}) = -£1.35$$

By contrast, the expected return on a £100 bet placed on one of the 36 numbers or on the zero may be calculated as:

$$(£100 \times \tfrac{1}{37} \times 35) + (-£100 \times \tfrac{36}{37}) = -£2.70$$

The mathematically expected loss on an even-money bet in single-zero roulette is 1.35 per cent, compared to a mathematically expected loss on any number of 2.70 per cent.

By the law of large numbers, the greater the number of spins of the wheel, the more likely it is that the gambler's actual win or loss will approximate the mathematical expectation. And since the expectation for both even-money bets and bets on individual numbers is negative – that is, the gambler expects to lose money – it is a bet that no professional gambler would place.

It should be noted that this negative expectation is due to the presence of the zero on the roulette wheel. Without a zero, the mathematical expectation of a £100 bet on an even-money chance would reduce to:

$$(£100 \times \tfrac{18}{36}) + (-£100 \times \tfrac{18}{36}) = £0$$

That is, the gambler would expect, on average, neither to win nor to lose, but to break even. This is a fair game where the monetary return offered to the gambler is exactly equal to the true odds of the outcome of that game, so the gambler is not placed at a disadvantage.

The extent to which the actual result may diverge from the expected result is defined by de Moivre's theorem. This theorem states that the actual results of a game tend to converge to the mathematically expected result as a function of the square root of the number of plays.

In 100 spins of a roulette wheel, we *expect* the ball to land on roughly $(\tfrac{18}{37} \times 100)$ = 49 red numbers; on $(\tfrac{18}{37} \times 100)$ = 49 black numbers; and on $(\tfrac{1}{37} \times 100)$ = 2 zeros. However, the actual results are likely to diverge from these expected returns quite significantly in any actual series of 100 trials.

De Moivre's theorem enables us to calculate the extent of this divergence as follows. The standard deviation of a series of results from their mathematical expectation within a Bernoulli process is given by the formula:

$$SD = \sqrt{n \times p \times q}$$

where SD = the standard deviation

n = the number of trials

p = the probability of occurrence of the event being studied in any individual trial

q = the probability of non-occurrence of the event being studied in any individual trial

$p + q$ = 1 in a Bernoulli process.

From the formula, the standard deviation for a red or black number in 100 spins of a roulette wheel may be calculated as:

$$SD = \sqrt{100 \times \tfrac{18}{37} \times \tfrac{19}{37}} = \sqrt{25} = 5$$

An approximation often used for the standard deviation of an even-money chance in a casino game is:

$$SD = \frac{\sqrt{n}}{2}$$

This approximation could be used to find the standard deviation of a red or black number in roulette, or punto or banco in baccarat, or a win for the player or the dealer in blackjack. It is not absolutely accurate mathematically, but represents a reasonable approximation of the correct formula. It is derived as follows. In a completely fair game, such as a roulette game without a zero, $p = q = 0.5$ for an even-money bet, and $p + q = 1$. There is a 50 per cent chance of a red or black, or even or odd number coming up. With a pay-off of 1 unit for every unit bet, the pay-off corresponds with the mathematical odds. For an event with a 50 per cent probability of occurring, the standard deviation is:

$$SD = \sqrt{n \times p \times q} = \sqrt{n \times 0.5 \times 0.5} = \sqrt{n \times 0.25}$$

The square root of 0.25 is 0.5, or one-half, so the standard deviation may be approximated by the formula $\sqrt{n}$ divided by 2.

In terms of money or bet units, the standard deviation is $(\sqrt{n}/2) \times$ number of bet units placed on each trial.

The true mathematical probability that an even-money chance in roulette will occur is actually slightly less than 0.5 ($\frac{18}{37} = 0.4865$), but it is close enough for $\sqrt{n}/2$ to be a valid approximation.

The standard deviation defines the likely range within which actual results will fall around their mathematical expectation. For 68.3 per cent of the time, the actual results will fall within one standard deviation of the expected outcome, and for 95 per cent of the time the actual results will fall within two standard deviations of the expected outcome. For 99.7 per cent of the time, the actual results will fall within three standard deviations of the mathematically expected outcome.

In the case of an even-money chance in roulette, the expected outcome is that the ball will land on it on 49 out of 100 spins. There is a standard deviation of ± 5 from this result, so in 68.3 per cent of each series of 100 spins, an even-money chance should come up between $(49 - 5) = 44$ and $(49 + 5) = 54$ times. In 95 per cent of each series of 100 spins, or 19 times out of 20, an even-money chance should come up between $(49 - 10) = 39$ and $(49 + 10) = 59$ times.

Extending the analysis further, in 99.7 per cent of all trials the actual result should be within three standard deviations of the expected result; and in only 0.3 per cent of all trials – or once on every 333 occasions – will the result fall outside three standard deviations. So if a gambler notes than an even-money chance on the roulette wheel has failed to come up more than $(49 - 15) = 34$ times, or has come up more than $(49 + 15) = 64$ times in 100 spins of a roulette wheel, he or she has just seen a 333–1 chance come in. Since there are three separate even-money bets (red/black, odd/even, high/low), a particular even-money chance may fall outside these limits once in every $\frac{333}{3} = 111$ series of trials.

Armed with this knowledge, it is possible to infer the methods that might have been used by Jaggers at Monte Carlo and by Hibbs and Walford in Nevada when they sought to identify significant biases on a roulette wheel. They could have divided the wheel into six segments of six numbers each (recording the zeros separately). On any spin, there would be a theoretically equal chance of $\frac{6}{37}$, or 16.2 per cent, of the ball landing on any of these segments. In any series of 100 spins, the balls would be expected to land on each of the segments 16 or 17 times, and on the zero twice or three times. The standard deviation from this result for any segment would be:

$$\sqrt{100 \times \tfrac{6}{37} \times \tfrac{31}{37}} = \sqrt{13.59} = 3.69.$$

In other words, the ball should land on each segment at least $(16 - 3.69) = 12$ times approximately, and at most $(17 + 3.69) = 21$ times approximately in two-thirds of each series of 100 trials recorded.

Knowing that the actual result should fall within three standard deviations in 99.7 per cent of all trials, Jaggers and the Hibbs-Walford team would have been alert to occasions when this did not happen. In the case of a series of six numbers on the roulette wheel, three standard deviations is equal to $(3 \times 3.69) = 11$ times approximately in any series of 100 spins of the wheel. If the ball landed on any sextant less than $(16 - 11) = 5$ times, or more than $(17 + 11) = 28$ times, in 100 spins of the wheel, they would know that something rather unusual had occurred. If in 10 series of 100 spins of the wheel, the same thing happened on three occasions, there would be strong prima facie evidence of bias. By undertaking such an analysis, they would have had a good idea of whether or not there was a bias on a roulette wheel by the time it had been spun 1,000 times. It would probably take two or three evenings for a roulette wheel to be spun this number of times under actual casino conditions.

If no bias is indicated, the house edge will grind the gambler down as play goes on. Over 100 spins of the wheel, a gambler placing a flat bet of £100 per spin on even-money chances can expect to be down (£10,000 × −1.35%), or £135. De Moivre's theorem provides estimates of the deviations that would occur from this mathematically expected result. For two-thirds of the time, a gambler betting £100 on even-money chances on each spin of the wheel will have an actual return of between +£365 and −£635 over 100 spins of a single-zero roulette wheel. For one-sixth of the time, the gambler will be lucky and win more than £365; while for the remaining one-sixth of the time, he or she will be unlucky and lose more than £635.

A gambler backing individual numbers on the same basis will be likely to lose more. Placing 100 bets, a gambler placing a flat bet of £100 on 18 of the 37 numbers can expect to be down (£10,000 × −2.70%), or £270.

However, for bets on a single number, the standard deviation will be proportionately much greater than for bets on an even-money chance. The standard deviation for 100 independent bets on a single number is $\sqrt{100 \times \tfrac{1}{37} \times \tfrac{36}{37}}$ or 1.62. In 100 spins of the wheel, the roulette ball be expected to land on each number on the roulette wheel ($100 \times \frac{1}{37}$) or approximately 2.7 times. The standard deviation of 1.62 represents 60 per cent of the expected outcome, against 23 per cent for any series of six numbers and 10 per cent for an even-money chance over any series of 100 spins of the wheel.

Because of the higher standard deviation, fluctuations in the gambler's capital will be much greater than for wagers placed on even-money chances. Over 1,000 spins of the roulette wheel, the number of times a single number can be expected to come up is $1,000 \times \frac{1}{37}$ or 27. The standard deviation from this expected result is $\sqrt{1,000 \times \frac{1}{37} \times \frac{36}{37}}$, or 5.12. Thus, for two-thirds of the time, a single number can be expected to come between $(27 - 5) = 22$ times and $(27 + 5) = 32$ times in any series of 1,000 spins of the roulette wheel. For one-sixth of the time, the ball will land on the number less than 22 times; and for one-sixth of the time the ball will land on the number more than 32 times. A gambler placing 1,000 successive £100 wagers on a single number such as 8 can expect to lose £2,700 of the £100,000 of action. For one-sixth of the time, there will be a negative fluctuation of more than one standard deviation and the gambler will lose more than £20,000 when the number comes up less than 22 times. However, for a precisely symmetrical one-sixth of the time the gambler will experience a positive fluctuation of more than one standard deviation and win more than £15,000 when the number comes up more than 32 times.

These wide swings, and the far better percentage prospect of winning substantial sums over a short period, explain why true gamblers often seek to defy the long-run laws of probability by betting on single numbers rather than even-money chances in roulette.

Appendix II

Player Advantage in Casino Blackjack

The Principles of Basic Strategy

The game of blackjack is in essence a mathematical system played according to a set of consistent logical rules. There is an optimal strategy for play against a randomly shuffled deck or shoe of cards. This strategy maximizes the player's expectation of winning or minimizes the expectation of losing, and is known as the basic strategy for play.

Though basic strategy is not itself a winning strategy, it forms the basis of all winning strategies that have been devised and is therefore the first essential tool for beating the game. A basic strategy player will still labour under a disadvantage of between −0.5 and −1.0 per cent against the game as it is offered in Britain, but this is lower than the disadvantage in any other casino game and significantly better than the disadvantage of between −3.0 and −5.0 per cent suffered by the average blackjack player who relies on hunches.

The basic strategy for the British game is slightly different from the game played in Las Vegas and Atlantic City. There are two major rule variations which affect the optimal strategy for the British game. First, the dealer does not draw a second card until all players have completed their hands. Second, the player is only allowed to split cards of equal value once, and is not allowed to split 4s, 5s or 10s. However, the player is allowed to double down on a split hand if the second card gives him or her a 2-card hard total of 9, 10 or 11.

The principles of winning blackjack are the the same whatever the precise rules that apply. The first principle is that, in order to win, it is not enough merely to capitalize on good hands by doubling down or splitting when the opportunity arises. It is also necessary to minimize the damage done by poor hands totalling between 12 and 16 by drawing if the dealer shows a strong card – despite the fact that most of the time the player will bust, and the bet be lost before the dealer has to play his or her hand. This can be discouraging, particularly when a sequence of hands worth between 12 and 16 is dealt to the player. Nevertheless, if the optimal strategy calls for drawing to totals between 12 and 16, this is what the player must do, no matter many times it leads to a bust hand. In the long run, good luck and bad luck will cancel out, and a good player who draws to stiff totals (between 12 and 16) against a dealer's 7, 8, 9, 10 or ace will lose less money by doing so than a poor player who always stands on stiff totals.

Julian Braun computed the exact probabilities for the dealer to draw to different totals in millions of computer simulations. These probabilities are given in Table II.1. For example, if the dealer's first card is a 4, then the dealer has a chance of 60 per cent of drawing to a pat hand (between 17 and 21), against a 40 per cent chance of busting. The player can expect to win most of the time against a dealer's 4 if he or she reaches a total of 18. To be precise, a total of 18 against a dealer's 4 will win outright 53 per cent of the time; tie 12 per cent of the time; and lose 35 per cent of the time (*How to Play Winning Blackjack*).

The worst cards for the dealer to show from the player's point of view are an ace or a 10. In both cases, the player needs to draw to 21 to be likely to win, or 20 to tie.

A player can expect to draw a stiff hand with a total of between 12 and 16 more than 40 per cent of the time. Such a hand will normally lose. In such circumstances, the player must weigh up the alternative of standing or drawing in order to establish which has the lesser expectation of loss.

For example, drawing to 16 against a dealer's 7 will lose the player less than the alternative of standing. Both are losing strategies (the player with a stiff hand of 16 is, unhappily, in a no-win situation whatever the dealer shows), but the

TABLE II.1

Probabilities that the dealer will draw to a given total with different initial cards (%) (Adapted from Julian Braun, *How to Play Winning Blackjack*)

Dealer's probability of drawing to:	Dealer shows:								*10	*♠
	2	3	4	5	6	7	8	9	10	♠
17	14	14	13	12	17	37	13	12	12	18
18	14	13	12	12	10	14	36	12	12	19
19	13	12	12	12	11	8	13	35	12	19
20	12	12	12	11	10	8	7	12	37	19
21	12	12	11	11	10	7	7	6	4	8
Bust	35	37	40	42	42	26	24	23	23	17
Player will win >50% if he draws to:	19	18	18	18	18	18	19	20	20	20

*10 includes court cards: King, Queen and Jack. Probabilities for 10 and ace are for cases where the dealer does not have a blackjack.

player who draws to 16 against a dealer's 7 can expect to win 29.5 out of every 100 hands, while the player who stands on 16 against 7 will win only 26 out of every 100 hands when the dealer busts. Thus, the option of drawing to 16 against 7 has a mathematically expected return which is 3.5 per cent greater than the alternative of standing.

Similar estimates have been computed for each of the player's options for drawing, doubling or splitting. These computations define the basic playing strategy for blackjack as played in British casinos.

The Player's Basic Strategy for Drawing and Standing

Hard hands

Hard hands are hands not containing an ace, or containing an ace which can only be valued as 1 if the value of the hand is not to exceed 21. The optimal playing rules for such hands are as follows:

1 Always draw on hard hands of value 11 or less.
   Rationale: you cannot bust by drawing, but can get closer to a value of 21.
2 Always stand on hard hands of value 17 or more.
   Rationale: the probability of going bust outweighs any additional return from improving the hand further without exceeding 21.
3 On hands of value 12, draw if the dealer's first card is 2 or 3, or 7 to ace; stand only if the dealer's first card is 4, 5 or 6.
   Rationale: the chance of going bust by drawing on 12 is 30.7 per cent (which is the probability of drawing a card with a value of 10), so in most cases it is worth drawing to try to improve the hand. However, if the dealer has a 4, 5 or 6, there is a good chance that the dealer will go bust; so the player's best option is to stand against these cards.
4 On hard hands with a value between 13 and 16, draw if the dealer's first card is between 7 and 10 or an ace; stand if the dealer's first card is between 2 and 6.
   Rationale: as for totals of 12 (see 3 above), but it is not worth the player's while to draw against 2 or 3 because of the greater probability of going bust with a stiff hand between 13 and 16. If the player draws to 13, his chance of going bust is 38.5 per cent, which is the probability of drawing a card with a value of 9 or 10. The probability of a bust increases if the player is drawing to a hand with a value of 14, 15 or 16. However, it is still worth taking the risk of drawing against a dealer's 7, 8, 9, 10 or ace, because of the probability with these cards that the dealer will draw to a pat hand (a hand of value 17 to 21), and will only pay players with a hand of greater value.

Soft hands

Soft hands are hands that include an ace which can be valued either 1 or 11 without the hand being bust. The rules for playing such hands are as follows:

1   Always draw on soft hands with a value of 17 (ace–6) or less.
2   Always stand on soft hands with a value of 19 (ace–8) or more.
3   Stand on soft hands with a value of 18 (ace–7) if the dealer's up card is between 2 and 8, or an ace; but draw on ace–7 if the dealer's up card is 9 or 10.

   Rationale: if the dealer is showing a card with a value between 2 or 8, the player holding ace–7 already has a strong hand which is likely to win or tie, as indicated by Julian Braun's computations in Table II.1, and there is no point in jeopardizing it by drawing. However, if the dealer shows 9 or 10, the probability is that the final value of the dealer's hand will be 19 or more, so the player with ace–7 holds a losing hand, and can improve his chances of winning by drawing. There is a probability of 53.8 per cent that the player will draw a 10, ace, 2 or 3, which will leave his hand no worse than it would be without drawing; while in the 46.2 per cent of cases where the player's hand is made worse by drawing, there is a chance that the dealer will still not be able to beat it. Julian Braun's computations indicate the player will enhance his expectation by 8 per cent by drawing rather than standing on ace–7 against 9, and by 4 per cent by drawing on ace–7 against 10. The question of whether to draw on ace–7 against a dealer's ace is a very fine one: the rule is to draw if the true count is negative, but not otherwise. The basic strategy player who does not count the cards is better off standing by a very slight margin.

The Player's Optimal Strategy for Doubling Down

The optimal strategy for doubling the original bet is as follows:

1   Double on 9 if the dealer's up card is 3, 4, 5 or 6.
2   Double on hard 10 or 11 if the dealer's up card is between 2 and 9.

Note: in American blackjack, the player is recommended to double on 11 against a dealer's 10. However, this is not optimal under British rules where the dealer collects all bets if the second card results in a dealer blackjack. Under British rules, if a player doubles on 11 and the dealer then draws an ace to his 10, the player would lose his entire bet and not merely the original stake as in the USA.

The Player's Optimal Strategy for Splitting

The optimal strategy for splitting two cards of equal value is as follows:

1   Split aces against all dealer cards except against a dealer's ace.
2   Split 8s against all dealer cards except against a dealer's 10 or ace.

3   Split 2s and 3s if the dealer's up card is between 2 and 7.

4   Split 6s if the dealer's up card is between 2 and 6.

5   Split 7s if the dealer's up card is between 2 and 7.

6   Split 9s if the dealer's up card is between 2 and 6, or 8 or 9, but *not* if the dealer's up card is 7. The reason for not splitting 9s against a dealer's 7 is that two 9s, with a value of 18, is already a winning hand against 7. From the table of dealer's probabilities (Table II.1), it will be seen that a dealer holding a 7 as his first card will draw to 17 for 37 per cent of the time and will bust for 26 per cent of the time. Thus, the player holding 18 against a dealer's 7 will win 63 per cent of the time. He will tie 14 per cent of the time, when the dealer also draws to 18; and only lose 23 per cent of the time, when the dealer draws to 19, 20 or 21.

Note: Splitting cards is optimal more often in British than in American blackjack, because in Britain, unlike in most casinos in the United States, the player is allowed to double down after splitting, thus reinforcing his advantage if the dealer shows a weak up card.

The Player's Optimal Strategy for Insurance

The optimal playing rule here is simple: a player who does not count the cards should never insure.

This counter-intuitive result was proved mathematically by Dr Edward Thorp in *Beat the Dealer*. Many players in British casinos accept the offer of insurance when they have a blackjack and the dealer shows an ace, because it seems to be a bet they cannot lose. In fact, it is a bad bet: while it cannot lose, it does not stand to win as much as the alternative of *not* taking insurance and being paid 3–2 if the dealer does not have a blackjack.

The reasoning is as follows. Of every £100 bet in which a player insures a blackjack, he would win £100 (insurance effectively paying even money whatever the dealer's second card). On the other hand, if the player never insured, the dealer would on average turn up a blackjack 30.7 per cent of the time, because that is the probability that the dealer will draw a 10. In this case, a tie results, with the player retaining his bet. On the other hand, in the remaining 69.3 per cent of cases where the dealer fails to draw a 10 to his ace, the player is paid at odds of 3–2: that is, he would be paid £103.95 (=£69.3 × $\frac{3}{2}$). Thus, the option of refusing insurance has a mathematically expected return which is £3.95 better for every £100 wagered than the option of accepting insurance.

The basic strategy is summarized in Table II.2.

Index: x = Stand, D = Draw, s = Split, BB = Double

TABLE II.2
Basic strategy for playing blackjack under British casino rules
1 Drawing and Standing (hard hands)

Player has:	Dealer shows:									
	2	3	4	5	6	7	8	9	10	♠
12	D	D	X	X	X	D	D	D	D	D
13	X	X	X	X	X	D	D	D	D	D
14	X	X	X	X	X	D	D	D	D	D
15	X	X	X	X	X	D	D	D	D	D
16	X	X	X	X	X	D	D	D	D	D
17	X	X	X	X	X	X	X	X	X	X

Drawing and standing (soft hands): *On soft hands, the player should stand on ace–7 versus a dealer's 2, 3, 4, 5, 6, 7, 8 or ace; and stand on ace–8 versus a dealer's 9 and 10.*

2 Splitting

Player has:	Dealer shows:									
	2	3	4	5	6	7	8	9	10	♠
ace-ace	S	S	S	S	S	S	S	S	S	D
2–2	S	S	S	S	S	S	D	D	D	D
3–3	S	S	S	S	S	S	D	D	D	D
6–6	S	S	S	S	S	D	D	D	D	D
7–7	S	S	S	S	S	S	D	D	D	D
8–8	S	S	S	S	S	S	S	S	D	D
9–9	S	S	S	S	S	X	S	S	X	X

3 Doubling

Player has:	Dealer shows:									
	2	3	4	5	6	7	8	9	10	♠
9	D	BB	BB	BB	BB	D	D	D	D	D
10	BB	BB	BB	BB	BB	BB	BB	BB	D	D
11	BB	BB	BB	BB	BB	BB	BB	BB	D	D

4 Insurance: *Do not take insurance.*

Concluding Comments on Basic Strategy

It is imperative that anyone who plans to play casino blackjack knows basic strategy by heart, and applies it. Any other strategy is inferior to basic, unless the player counts the cards. Learning and applying basic strategy is likely to be the most rewarding investment that a casino gambler can make. Playing basic strategy will negate most of the advantage that the dealer enjoys in the game of blackjack by virtue of drawing last.

Basic strategy will not eliminate the dealer's advantage entirely. If the player sticks to basic strategy without variation, the dealer's advantage will be reduced to an average of just under 1 per cent throughout all shoes. That is, of every £100 staked by the player, the player would on average lose just under £1. This represents the best bet available to a casino gambler who does not count cards. It is significantly better than backing an even-money chance on the roulette wheel. It is also superior to the best bets available in baccarat (punto banco) or craps.

Furthermore, although basic strategy does not of itself constitute a winning system, it is the foundation of all winning systems in blackjack. Even the most skilful player is likely to employ basic strategy nine-tenths of the time. The playing strategy will be varied from basic only on rare occasions; and the variations can best be comprehended in relation to basic strategy.

The odds can be improved if the player *counts* the cards, and can tell roughly when the shoe is in the player's favour, and when it is in the dealer's favour. If the player counts accurately, and increases the bet when the probabilities are in his favour, he or she can actually gain a slight edge over the dealer.

The Theory of Card Counting

The blackjack player who masters the basic strategy will be capable of playing the game better than nine out of ten players in Britain. The bad news is that, despite this, the basic strategy player will lose in the long run, at a rate approaching £10 for every £1,000 wagered. These losses will not be smooth: there will be frequent winning sessions, interspersed with slightly more frequent losing sessions. But over a long enough period, the disadvantage of just under 1 per cent suffered by the basic strategy player will be decisive. The fact that the basic strategist will be losing less than other players who rely on hunches will not be much consolation.

However, there is some good news. The losses are not inevitable. They can be turned into profits if one vital piece of information can be gleaned. That piece of information is what cards are most likely to be dealt next, based on the cards that have already been dealt from the deck or shoe of cards.

Julian Braun simulated the effects on the player's advantage of removing different cards from a standard deck. Later, John Gwynn, Armand Seri and

Peter Griffin of California State University, Sacramento, estimated the effects by linear approximation, applying the method of least squares. Their results are given in Table II.3 below.

TABLE II.3

Effects of removing all cards of a given value from a standard deck on the player's advantage (disadvantage) in casino blackjack (rounded to the second decimal point).

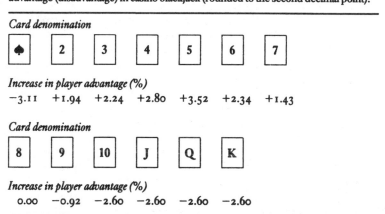

Card denomination

♠	2	3	4	5	6	7

Increase in player advantage (%)

−3.11	+1.94	+2.24	+2.80	+3.52	+2.34	+1.43

Card denomination

8	9	10	J	Q	K

Increase in player advantage (%)

0.00	−0.92	−2.60	−2.60	−2.60	−2.60

It will be noted from Table II.3 that the best card to remove, from the player's point of view, is the 5. If all 5s were removed fom the deck, the player's advantage against the dealer would increase by 3.52 per cent compared to the advantage that would pertain with a complete deck. What this means is that, if the player had a starting advantage of −0.65 per cent using basic strategy (the approximate percentage under British rules), it would increase to (3.52 − 0.65 per cent) = +2.87 per cent if all sixteen 5s were removed from a four-deck shoe.

By contrast, if all the aces were removed, the player's advantage would fall by 3.11 per cent, so the aggregate disadvantage would be (−3.11 − 0.65 per cent) = −3.76 per cent. With four 10s removed from a standard 52-card deck, the player's advantage would fall by 2.6 per cent.

The total of all the positive and negative effects sum to zero, which implies that, if equal numbers of cards of each denomination are removed, the shoe returns to the original 'off the top' advantage or disadvantage. The effect is the same as if the player is playing against a complete randomly shuffled deck of cards.

Alternative Counting Systems

The purpose of a counting system is to enable the player to keep track of the cards as they are dealt, in order to adjust the bet size and playing strategy accordingly. A number of systems have been developed since Thorp's seminal *Beat the Dealer*, which assign a positive value to low cards, to indicate that the player's advantage rises when they are discarded, and a negative value to high cards, to indicate that the player's advantage falls when they are discarded.

The card counter keeps a single cumulative running count in mind at all times, and adjusts it to the true count by dividing by the number of decks still to be dealt. With a running count of +9, and three decks still to be dealt, the true count would be $+\frac{9}{3} = +3$. The true count provides the counter with a mental picture of the structure of the cards still to be dealt.

Table II.4 summarizes a number of different systems for counting the cards which have been devised over the last 30 years. They all assign negative values to high cards (10s) to indicate that the player's advantage falls as these cards are removed, and positive values to low cards (3 to 6) to indicate that the player's advantage rises as these cards are removed. It will be noted that those counts which assign a negative value to the ace have a higher betting efficiency but lower playing efficiency that those which assign a zero value to the ace. The reason is that the ace is a high card for betting purposes (assisting the player) but a low card for playing purposes (as a player can never be busted by drawing an ace). It will also be noted that more complex systems are not significantly more efficient in either betting or playing terms than the better simple systems such as hi-opt I.

The Main Count System

The main count is one of the most efficient counting systems for both betting and playing decisions. There are more efficient systems for either playing or betting, but in order to use these the player would have to keep two counts running in his head simultaneously during a game, as well as making the necessary adjustments from the running count to the true count. The greater complexity of such calculations inevitably increases the risk that the player will make significant errors in his counting, and consequently in his betting and playing strategies.

Under the main count system, the following values are assigned to each of the cards:

Card	2	3	4	5	6	7	8	9	10	ace
Point count	+1	+1	+2	+2	+2	+1	0	0	−2	−1

If a deck of cards is counted down accurately, applying these values to each card as it is dealt, the final count will be zero when the last card is dealt, because the

TABLE II.4
The comparative efficiency of different counting systems

System	Card point counts:										Efficiencies for:	
	2	3	4	5	6	7	8	9	10	♠	Betting	Playing
Braun/Dubner hi-lo	1	1	1	1	1	0	0	0	−1	−1	0.97	0.510
Einstein (hi-opt I)	0	1	1	1	1	0	0	0	−1	0	0.88	0.615
Revere plus-minus	1	1	1	1	1	0	0	−1	−1	0	0.89	0.592
Thorp	1	1	1	1	1	1	0	−1	−1	−1	0.96	0.532
Gordon/DHM	1	1	1	1	0	0	0	0	−1	0	0.86	0.574
Uston plus-minus	0	1	1	1	1	1	0	0	−1	−1	0.95	0.547
Revere point count	1	2	2	2	2	1	0	0	−2	−2	0.98	0.527
Hi-opt II	1	1	2	2	1	1	0	0	−2	0	0.91	0.671
Main (zen) count	1	1	2	2	2	1	0	0	−2	−1	0.97	0.630
Uston APC	1	2	2	3	2	2	1	−1	−3	0	0.91	0.690
Revere APC − 1971	2	3	3	4	3	2	0	−1	−3	−4	1.00	0.523
Revere APC − 1973	2	2	3	4	2	1	0	−2	−3	0	0.92	0.657
Ten count	4	4	4	4	4	4	4	4	−9	4	0.72	0.621

Sources: Adapted from Peter Griffin, *The Theory of Blackjack*, Chapter 4; Humble and Cooper, *The World's Greatest Blackjack Book*, Chapter 8; and 'The "Best" Card Counting System', *Blackjack Forum*, vol. I, no. 3, September 1981

number of cards with positive values is exactly equal to the number of cards with negative values. However, at any point during the deal, the running count is likely to deviate from zero. If this deviation is large, the player can assess whether he or the dealer has an edge, based on a prediction of whether the cards remaining to be dealt will be predominantly high in value (10, ace), or low in value (between 2 and 7).

The running count is calculated as an absolute number. However, since the cards are dealt from a shoe containing four decks, the significance of this absolute number changes as the number of cards dealt increases. For example, if there is a running count of +15 after the first hand of a shoe is dealt, its significance is far less than if the running count is +15 as the last deck is dealt. The relative excess of 10s is far less in the former case.

In order to convert the running count into a true count which accurately reflects the significance of the count at that stage of the shoe, the player needs to apply the following calculation:

$$\text{True count} = \frac{\text{running count}}{\text{number of decks to be dealt}}$$

In the case of a four-deck shoe, the true count can be calculated with sufficient accuracy by dividing the running count by four at early in the deal; by three once approximately one pack (52 cards) has been dealt; and by two once approximately two packs (104 cards) have been dealt. With practice, a player can estimate the number of decks dealt by a glance at the discard shoe to the dealer's right, where all hands that have been played are placed.

Learning to Count

Learning how to keep an accurate running count requires several hours of practice. A player should start with a deck of 52 cards, counting each down slowly one by one, and ensuring that the final count after the last card is dealt is zero. Accuracy is more important than speed; speed will come with practice. In order to keep an accurate running count under casino conditions, where dealers deal quite rapidly and there are many distractions, the player should be able to count down a deck of 52 cards in 20 seconds or less, and four decks in no more than 90 seconds. A player who cannot accurately count down a deck in less than 30 seconds, or four decks in less than two minutes, is likely to be in severe difficulty under actual casino conditions, and will be liable to lose the count quite often.

In view of the casinos' policy of barring any suspected card counter, the card count should be kept mentally and no indication should be given that the player is counting.

In order to count down rapidly, the player must keep count of the cards in groups of two or three. Counting in groups of three requires that the player instantly recognizes the value of three-card combinations, such as the following:

Combination	Running count
4 4 6	+6
5 3 ace	+2
7 10 queen	−3
8 9 2	+1
ace king jack	−5
5 2 10	+1
6 10 jack	−2

Someone learning to count the cards should count one card after another to begin with, and try to reduce the time taken to count down a deck from 90 seconds to 60 and then 30 seconds. This will require many hours of practice.

If a player does not have the dedication or self-displine to learn to count cards at this speed, he or she can still enjoy the game socially by employing basic strategy. Similarly, if the player loses count, he or she should revert to playing basic strategy for the rest of that shoe, before trying to pick up the count again on the next shoe. In these circumstances, the player will be playing at a disadvantage of less than 1 per cent, so losing count is not the end of the world.

Above all, a novice card counter should not panic or seek to guess the count. Every winning player has gone through a period of dropping the count, and as long as the player knows basic strategy and bets only the table minimum, not too much damage will be suffered. Alternatively, the player can stop and have a coffee or move to another table. You do not have to play on when you have dropped the count, nor do you have to play on if the count is very negative, indicating that the dealer has a large edge over the players. One of the few advantages possessed by the player is that he or she need only play when in peak condition, and can choose to stop at any time. The dealer has to go on dealing, whether or not the cards are good for the house.

Once the player knows basic strategy and how to count the cards, he or she will have laid the foundations of winning blackjack. Upon these foundations can be built a strategy for betting and playing which can give the player an edge over the casino.

Betting Strategy

In theory, anyone who knows basic strategy and who has trained themselves to keep an accurate count of the cards dealt can become a winning blackjack player.

Most card counters do not win over the long haul. There are a number of reasons for this. First, card counters make mistakes. They may count wrongly or make an error in play. The longer a playing session goes on, the more tired the counter becomes, and the more likely it is that he or she will make mistakes. For this reason, many winning card counters do not play for more than half an hour or 45 minutes at a time. Second, card counters may play in conditions that cannot be beaten: where the table is crowded, for example, or where the cut card is inserted high in a shoe. Third, card counters may lack patience and start to chase the cards, by increasing the bet too steeply when the true count becomes positive. Winning blackjack is a long, hard grind where the odds are seldom in the player's favour, and the player is usually losing small amounts. When the cards turn slightly in the player's favour, there is a temptation to chase them by steaming up the bets in an effort to recoup all the accumulated losses in one winning coup. This temptation must be avoided.

The most important single factor in beating the game of blackjack is money management. The British game cannot be consistently beaten by a player who places flat bets on each hand, no matter how skilful the variation in playing strategy. The mathematics of the game militate against it. Even the most skilful player cannot expect to win more than 48 per cent of the hands dealt, against 52 per cent for the dealer, because of the crucial advantage possessed by the dealer in drawing last. It is therefore essential for the player to increase the size of his or her bet in the minority of favourable situations. Conversely, if the true count is 3 or less, the player should bet his minimum stake.

The theoretically optimal bet size was defined by J. L. Kelly in a paper entitled 'A New Interpretation of Information Rate', where he set out a rule which has since become very popular with gamblers. The Kelly criterion states that a gambler should bet the *same percentage of his bankroll as the estimated percentage advantage he enjoys*. A gambler who follows this rule will maximize his rate of gain. Formally, the Kelly optimal bet may be defined as

$$b^* = (p - q) B$$

where b^* = the value of the optimal bet

p = the probability of success

q = the probability of failure

$(p + q)$ = 1 or 100 per cent; and

B = total value of the gambler's bankroll

For example, in a moderately favourable situation in blackjack where $p = 0.505$ and $q = 0.495$ approximately, giving the player an edge of 0.01, then the player's optimal bet with a 1,000 unit bankroll would be (1,000 × 0.01), or 10 units.

It is not possible in practice to precisely apply the Kelly criterion in casino blackjack, for two main reasons. First, for most of the time the player does not have a mathematical advantage. Under such circumstances, the Kelly criterion would recommend a negative bet. But the player cannot place a negative bet in practice. The player could drop out of the game if the true count was negative; but if a player persistently drops out and then returns when the true count turns positive, he would both irritate other players and attract the attention of the pit boss. Consequently, consistently dropping out of play on negative counts is not a feasible strategy. The player must place a minimum bet in order to stay in the game, even when the odds are in the dealer's favour.

A second practical difficulty with the Kelly criterion is that the player is unlikely to be able to compute either the exact size of his bankroll, or the exact percentage advantage, before any hand is dealt. The size of the bankroll constantly fluctuates from one hand to another, as does the player's advantage or disadvantage.

A further difficulty with the Kelly criterion is that it does not take account of standard deviation. The player will place many small bets that collectively will have a low standard deviation, and a few high bets that will have a high standard deviation. For this reason, Joel Friedman, in a paper presented to the Fifth National Conference on Gambling and Risk Taking, recommended betting only between 50 and 80 per cent of the level advised by a strict Kelly system. He found that pursing such a strategy would significantly cut the fluctuations in a gambler's return but only slightly reduce the rate of return.

I would support Joel Friedman's recommendations for two further reasons. First, a few very high bets are likely to attract casino attention and significantly increase the risk of being barred. Second, even experts disagree on the extent of the advantage possessed by the player at any true count. In an important but neglected paper entitled 'How True is your True Count?', Arnold Snyder and John Gwynn published the results of extensive computer simulations of the player's advantage at a wide range of true counts which showed only an erratic relationship between them.

I will advance my own theory of the reasons for this result later in the Appendix. The point here is that the Snyder/Gwynn results should caution any blackjack player against too rigid an application of the Kelly betting system.

A betting scheme I have used successfully on medium and high stakes tables is as follows:

True count	Bet units	Average % of play	Approximate % edge	1,000 hands	
				Expected win	Standard deviation
TC < 4	1	79	− 1.0	− 7.9	14
3 < TC < 8	4	12	+ 1.0	+ 4.8	22
7 < TC < 10	8	6	+ 2.0	+ 9.6	31
TC > 9	12	3	+ 3.0	+ 10.8	33
		100	+ 0.8	+ 17.3	

The standard deviation is estimated by using the approximation of $(\sqrt{n}/2) \times$ number of bet units placed on each trial, the derivation of which was explained in Appendix I.

Thus, in any series of 1,000 hands, on average 79 per cent or 790 bets will be placed of 1 unit each when the true count is less than 4. The standard deviation of these bets is $(\sqrt{790}/2) \times 1$, or $\frac{28}{2}$, or 14 bet units. In the 12 per cent of cases when the true count lies between 4 and 7, 4 bet units are wagered, and the standard deviation of these bets is $(\sqrt{120}/2) \times 4$, or 22 bet units. A similar methodology is applied to calculate the standard deviation of the bets placed at higher true count levels.

It will be noted that the standard deviation of the less frequent large bets placed at high true counts is higher than that of the more frequent small bets placed at low true counts. In other words, the monetary fluctuations experienced by a gambler placing a few bets will be greater than those of a gambler wagering a similar total amount of money in many small bets.

Using this betting scheme, a player expects to put 2,110 bet units into action over 1,000 hands of play and win 17 units; a win rate of approximately 0.8 per cent of all money gambled. It takes between 7 and 10 hours to play out 1,000 hands. The standard deviation of 100 bet units implies that for two-thirds of the time the gambler will achieve an actual result of between −83 units (17 − 100) and +117 units (17 + 100). For the remaining one-third of the time, the actual result will lie outside these limits.

Unless a gambler is playing for fun, pursuing this scheme is not likely to be worthwhile for stakes of less than £25 per hand, on which the expected win rate is £425 over 1,000 hands, with a standard deviation of £2,500. The maximum bet at the £25 level would be 12 × £25 or £300 at very high true counts. A bankroll of £7,500 approximately (300 units) would be required to withstand a negative fluctuation of more than two standard deviations, which will occur once in every 20 sequences of 1,000 hands played. To be safe, a gambler pursuing this betting scheme should have a bankroll of 400 units, or £10,000 at the £25 level. Mathematically, the gambler would have to play almost 25,000 hands of cards to double this initial bankroll (= 1,000 × 400 / 17.3), which could be expected to require between 200 and 250 hours of play. A player who played solidly for six hours, day after day, in order to achieve this target would need to play for about 40 days to win £10,000.

These theoretical conclusions are confirmed by my own empirical research at the blackjack table.

My experience also indicates that the win rate achieved under actual casino conditions is likely to be less than the mathematically expected win. This is because of human error and because, in practice, there are constraints on the bet spread that it is possible for a gambler to use. A player at the £25 tables who suddenly increased his bet to £200 or £300 would soon be noticed by casino personnel and barred.

With a lower bet spread, or a smaller bankroll, the win rate is lower and the risk of ruin higher. The risk of ruin in a positive expectation game is defined by the formula

$$R = \frac{q}{p}^{B}$$

where R = the risk of ruin

q = the probability of failure on any single trial

p = the probability of success on any single trial

B = the gambler's initial bankroll in units

For example, if a gambler participates in a game where he or she enjoys a 1 per cent edge, then $q = 0.495$ and $p = 0.505$. With a bankroll of only 1 unit ($B = 1$), $R = \frac{0.495}{0.505} = 0.98$. That is, there is a probability of 98 per cent that the gambler will eventually be ruined even though he or she is playing with a positive mathematical expectation. With two units, the risk of ruin falls to ($\frac{0.495}{0.505}$ squared), or approximately 96 per cent. With a bankroll of 20 units, the risk of ruin falls to ($\frac{0.495}{0.505}$) multiplied by itself 20 times, or approximately 67 per cent; with 50 units it falls to 37 per cent; with 100 units to 13.5 per cent; with 200 units to 1.8 per cent; and with 300 units to 0.25 per cent.

It can be seen from the formula that the risk of ruin will be lower the greater the gambler's initial edge (i.e. the lower the ratio q/p), and the larger the gambler's initial bankroll (B).

A commonly accepted risk of ruin is 5 per cent, or 1 in 20. To have a 5 per cent risk of ruin in a game where he enjoys a 1 per cent edge, the gambler requires a bankroll of 150 units. In the case of blackjack, a larger bankroll is required because blackjack is a complex mathematical system in which the gambler's edge is not constant. Most of the time the gambler is playing with a negative expectation; he grinds ahead by betting more in the minority of cases where he enjoys a positive expectation. It will be noted that the bankroll of 400 units suggested for a 1–4–8–12 betting scheme represents only 100 4-unit bets.

Variations in Playing Strategy

So far, card counting has been considered only as a means of identifying favourable situations for the player which can be used to bet more heavily when the odds are in the player's favour. However, the true count is also used by skilful players to vary playing strategy from basic. Although basic strategy is the most efficient strategy for the player to apply against a randomly shuffled deck of 52 cards, it becomes increasingly inefficient the further the true count diverges from zero.

Most established systems for counting the cards have a greater betting efficiency than playing efficiency. The main count used in this Appendix is among the most efficient systems for both betting and playing, with a betting efficiency of approximately 95 per cent and a playing efficiency of approximately 65 per cent. Commenting on this count system, Arnold Snyder wrote in the September 1981 edition of *Blackjack Forum*: 'I could find no significantly better count than this count, in which the ace, valued as −1, is not neutralized (valued 0) but half neutralized. In other words, I have taken the middle road – a zen approach. It is this trick which keeps the betting efficiency high while maintaining a very respectable playing efficiency.' Subsequent computer tests by John Gwynn and Armand Seri of California State University, Sacramento, have confirmed the robustness of the system.

Table II.5 provides detailed variations in playing strategy using the main count system. The table provides the critical indices or strike numbers at which a player should change basic strategy. The true count index at which the player's strategy should change for each combination of player's cards versus the dealer's up card is given in the corresponding square within the matrix.

For example, if the dealer has a 10 value card showing as his first card while the player has a total of 15, the player should draw another card if the true count is 6 or less, and stand if the true count is greater than 6. This result, and all the others shown in the matrices, was derived from many millions of computer simulations as that which offers the greatest expected return to the player.

TABLE II.5
Complete strategy tables for the main count: x = Stand, D = Draw, s = Split
1 Drawing and standing variations

You have:	Dealer shows:									
	2	3	4	5	6	7	8	9	10	♠
	Stand if the true count is greater than:									
12	5	3	−1	−3	−2	D	D	D	D	D
13	−2	−4	−6	−7	−8	D	D	D	D	D
14	−6	−8	−10	−12	−12	26	23	20	12	24
15	−11	−12	−14	−17	−17	17	15	13	6	16
16	−16	−18	−20	−24	−26	15	11	8	0	14
ace−7	x	x	x	x	x	x	x	D	D	1

2 Splitting variations

You have:	Dealer shows:									
	2	3	4	5	6	7	8	9	10	♠
	Split if the true count is greater than:									
2–2	−6	−9	−12	−15	S	S	10	D	D	D
3–3	−2	−12	S	S	S	S	D	D	D	D
6–6	−4	−7	−10	−13	S	D	D	D	D	D
7–7	S	S	S	S	S	S	2	D/X	D/X	D/X
8–8	S	S	S	S	S	S	S	S	D/X	D/X
9–9	−4	−6	−9	−12	−12	10	S	S	X	X
ace–ace	−22	−24	−26	−30	−32	−17	−15	−15	−13	D

3 Doubling variations

You have:	Dealer shows:									
	2	3	4	5	6	7	8	9	10	♠
	Double if the true count is greater than:									
9	2	−2	−5	−8	−11	7	14	D	D	D
10	−17	−19	−21	−25	−28	−13	−8	−3	D	D
11	−22	−25	−26	−30	−32	−18	−13	−8	10	D

4 Insurance variations

Insure if the true count is greater than +5

There is an internal logic to the critical indices, which may be summarized as follows.

As the true count goes down (i.e. becomes minus), it indicates that the proportion of low cards between 2 and 7 in the shoe goes up. Therefore the player's probability of busting to stiff totals of between 12 and 16 decreases, so the player should draw more than indicated by basic strategy – the drawing table indicates that the player's expectation is maximized by drawing to totals of 12

TABLE 11.6
A Simplified Playing Strategy (UK rules)

Exact count	Bet units	Playing	Splitting	Doubling	Insurance
Basic strategy Normal: −5 to +5	1	Draw to 11 vs. everything Draw to 12 vs. 2 or 3 Draw to 16 vs. 7, 8, 9, 10 or ace Draw to ace–6 vs. everything Draw to ace–7 vs. 9 or 10	Split 2s, 3s and 7s vs. 2–7 Split 6s vs. 2–6 Split 8s vs. 2–9 Split 9s vs. 2–9 except 7 Split aces vs. everything except aces	Double down 9 vs. 3–6 Double down 10 vs. 2–9 Double down 11 vs. 2–9	Do not insure
Basic strategy					
High counts Quite high: +6 to +10 Variations on basic	5	Don't draw to 12 vs. 2 or 3 Don't draw to 15 or 16 vs. 10 Don't draw to 16 vs. 9	Split 7s vs. 8	Double down 9 vs. 2 and 7	Take insurance
Very high: +11 to +15 Variations on basic	10	Don't draw to 16 vs. 8, 9 or 10 Don't draw to 15 vs. 9 or 10 Don't draw to 14 vs. 10	Split 7s vs. 8 Split 9s vs. 7s Split 2s vs. 8s	Double down 9 vs. 2 and 7	Take insurance

		Draw	Split	Double down	Insurance
Extremely high: > +15			Split 7s vs. 8 / Split 3s vs. 7s / Split 2s vs. 8s	Double down 9 vs. 2, 7 and 8	Take insurance
Variations on basic	15	Don't draw on 16 at all / Don't draw on 15 at all / Don't draw to 14 vs. 9, 10 or ace			
Low counts Low: −6 to −10	1				Do not insure
Variations on basic		Draw to 12 vs. everything / Draw to 13 vs. 2–4 / Draw to 14 vs. 2 / Draw to ace–7 vs. ace	Don't split 6s vs. 2 or 3 (draw instead) / Don't split 2s or 3s vs. 2 / Don't split 9s vs. 2 or 3 (stand instead)	Don't double down 9 except vs. 5 or 6 / Don't double down 10 vs. 9	
Very low: −11 to −15	1				Do not insure
Variations on basic		Draw to 12, 13, 14 vs. everything / Draw to 15 vs. 2 or 3 / Draw to ace–7 vs. ace	Don't split 9s except vs. 8 or 9 (stand) / Don't split 6s except vs. 5 or 6 (draw) / Don't split 2s or 3s except vs. 4–7	Don't double down on 9 at all / Don't double down 10 or 11 vs. 8 or 9 / Don't double down on 10 vs. 7	
Extremely low: < −15	1				Do not insure
Variations on basic		Draw to 12, 13, 14, 15 vs. everything / Draw to 16 vs. 2 or 3 / Draw to ace–7 vs. ace	Split 2 only vs. 6 or 7 / Split 3 only vs. 4–7 / Split 6s only vs. 6 / Split 9s only vs. 8 or 9 / Split aces only vs. 2–6	Don't double down on 9 at all / Don't double down 10 except vs. 3–6 / Don't double down 11 except vs. 2–6	

and 13 even against weak dealer cards such as 4, 5 or 6 if the true count falls to less than −8. Moreover, because the player's probability of drawing a high card diminishes, the player should also split and double less than indicated by basic strategy.

Conversely, as the true count rises, it indicates that the shoe is becoming richer in high cards, and consequently the player should draw less because the risk of busting rises. The player should split or double down more because the chances of drawing to a good total rise – and so does the dealer's chance of busting, because the dealer must draw to totals of between 12 and 16.

The indices in Table II.5 provide strike numbers for the true count at which the player should switch from playing according to basic strategy to an alternative strategy. Precise play according to the indices provided in the table is an ideal to which players should aspire.

In practice, it may be difficult for a player to adjust the playing strategy precisely according to these indices. There is also a very real risk, highlighted in a paper by Peter Griffin ('On the Likely Consequences of Errors in Card Counting'), that too frequent variations from basic strategy, compounded with marginal errors in counting or calculating the true count adjustment, can actually end up costing the player money.

Accordingly, it may be easier in practice to follow a simpler playing strategy with a few key strike numbers. The strategy outlined in Table II.6 involves only varying strategy of play at strike numbers of plus or minus 5, 10 and 15.

The Player's Mathematical Advantage in Blackjack

Little has been published on the effect appropriate variations in playing strategy may have on the player's mathematical advantage in blackjack.

Most of the literature on the game assumes that there is a linear relationship between the true count and the player's advantage (or disadvantage), of the form

$$y = a + bx$$

where y = the player's percentage advantage

x = the true count (= the running count of the cards dealt divided by the number of decks still to be dealt)

a = the player's advantage at the outset of play with a new shoe of cards when using the basic strategy for play (equal to approximately −0.65 per cent for casino blackjack played under British rules from a four-deck shoe of cards)

b = the extent to which the initial advantage varies with the true count.

In other words, the player's advantage or disadvantage is assumed to rise and fall proportionately with the true count.

Various estimates are given in the literature for the parameters *a* and *b*. The value of *a*, the intercept parameter, defines the per cent advantage that the player enjoys when play begins from a randomly shuffled deck or shoe of cards. It depends upon the number of decks used and the rules of play. This value has been computed as equal to −0.65 per cent for a player applying basic strategy under British rules with four decks, and +0.02 per cent under the best rules offered for one-deck blackjack on the Las Vegas Strip.

By comparison with the precision of the estimates for *a*, the estimates provided for the slope parameter *b* tend to be approximate. The value of *b* is reckoned to be the order of 0.5 for a one-level count such as hi-opt I, or 0.25 for a two-level count such as hi-opt II or the main count. Humble & Cooper give a more precise estimate for *b* of 0.515 using the hi-opt I method of counting the cards.

These estimates suggest a straight-line relationship between the true count and the player's advantage. Some authors qualify this by accepting that the true relationship is not exactly linear, but state that the assumption of linearity is accurate enough for practical purposes.

Utilizing a Kelly-optimal betting system, the skilful player seeking to maximize the expected return from the game would increase the bet as the true count rises, and decrease the bet as the true count falls. This procedure is universally recommended in the literature on blackjack, qualified only by the constraint placed on the speed and extent of bet variations by the possibility that the casino will bar the player.

Practical application of these methods in the casinos of Mayfair and Monte Carlo indicated to this researcher that they could be effective, but appeared to be sub-optimal. In particular, at very high counts the player advantage did not appear to be as great as indicated by the linear relationship specified in the equation $y = a + bx$.

The nature of the relationship between the true count and the player's advantage is discussed in Peter Griffin's *Theory of Blackjack*. Griffin opens Chapter 10 with the following comment:

Card counters are like the prototypical Don Juan who wants every woman he meets to succumb to him and then wishes to marry a virgin; they want all the 5s to be put out of the deck before they raise their bets and then they want the dealer to show one as an up card! There is an apparent paradox in that the cards whose removal most favours the player before the deal are also the cards whose appearance as the dealer's up card most favours the player.

Griffin goes on to calculate that the probability of a dealer bust is maximized when approximately 41 per cent of the remaining cards to be dealt are 10s. When the proportion of 10s rises above this, the dealer's chance of busting tends to fall, as it becomes more likely that the dealer will receive a pat hand of between 17 and 21 with the first two cards drawn.

In other words, the best situations for the player may occur, not at extremely high counts when most of the cards to be dealt are 10s, but rather at moderately high counts when there is a mix of high and low cards waiting to be dealt. This mix of high and low cards maximizes the chance that the dealer will bust, and that the player will be able to exploit favourable opportunities to split or double.

My conclusion is that the true relationship between the player's advantage and the true count is not linear but parabolic. With only 10s and court cards remaining in the shoe, the true count would be very high, but the player would enjoy no advantage whatever, because all hands would be tied. Conversely, at very low (negative) counts, a player would be at a greater disadvantage playing basic strategy than indicated by a simple linear relationship, because the majority of the player's splits and double downs would lose. Thus, the negative impact of the changing structure of the deck is reinforced by the increasing inefficiency of basic strategy as a method of play.

An approximation of the relationship between the player's advantage and the true count may be specified by a quadratic equation of the form

$$y = a + bx + cx^2$$

where y = the player's percentage advantage

x = the true count (= the running count of the cards dealt divided by the number of decks still to be dealt)

a = the player's advantage at the outset of play with a new shoe of cards when using basic strategy

b = the extent to which the initial advantage varies with the true count as a result of changes in the structure of the undealt cards

c = the extent to which the initial advantage varies with the true count as a result of changes in the efficiency of the playing strategy

The reason that the player's advantage is more accurately specified by a quadratic than a linear equation is that two things are changing as the cards are dealt out. One is the structure of the deck of cards remaining to be dealt. The other is the optimal strategy for play.

The effect of the changing structure is captured by the slope parameter b, which measures the positive impact of a higher true count on player advantage. The b parameter indicates that, as the cards remaining to be dealt become richer in high cards, so the player's advantage tends to rise, other things being equal.

But other things are not equal. Basic strategy becomes less and less accurate as a method of play, the further the true count diverges from zero. When the true count is negative, the player's disadvantage caused by the poorness of the deck is reinforced by the inadequacy of the playing strategy, so the total disadvantage is greater than would be measured in a linear relationship. Conversely, when the true count is positive and high, the advantage that the player derives from a rich deck is attenuated by the fact that basic strategy is no longer the most efficient method of play. The increasing inefficiency of basic strategy is proxied by the parameter c, which is negative.

With a two-level count such as the main count, the parameters have the following approximate values:

$a = -0.65$ under British rules
$b = +0.28$ using the true count indicated by the main count system
$c = -0.01$ applying basic strategy

The roots of the equation are given by the formula,

$$x_1, x_2 = \frac{-b \pm \sqrt{b^2 - 4ca}}{2c}$$

or, solving with the estimated parameters values above,

$$x_1, x_2 = \frac{-0.28 \pm \sqrt{0.0784 - (4 \times -0.01 \times -0.65)}}{2 \times -0.01}$$

The solution to this equation gives values for $y = 0$ when $x = 2.5$ or when $x = 25$. That is to say, the player is playing even with the dealer when the true count is 2.5, or when the true count is 25.

The result that the player enjoys an even game with the dealer at a slightly positive true count is well established. Less familiar is the result that the game is also even at very high counts. At a true count of 25, the deck would be largely composed of cards which would result in both the player and the dealer drawing to a pat hand on most deals of two cards, so either would have an equal chance of winning, and neither would enjoy an advantage.

It should be emphasized that the curve does not measure a precise, unique relationship between the true count and player advantage. At any true count, there are millions of possible card combinations waiting to be dealt, each with a different impact on the player's advantage relative to the dealer. The estimated relationship represents the best fit of all possible relative advantages at each count. Extensive computer simulations of the type undertaken by Braun and Griffin would be necessary to compute the full scatter; my estimates have been calculated using basic algebra and probability theory.

However, while the curve is not precise, it gives a reasonable estimate of the true advantage enjoyed during a long series of plays using basic strategy. In particular, the estimates are superior to estimates calculated on the basis of a linear relationship.

There are two implications of this curve which are worthy of comment. The first is that the player's *average* disadvantage applying basic strategy under British rules is not 0.65 per cent (the value of the intercept parameter), but somewhat higher. If the relationship between the true count and player advantage *were* linear, then the average disadvantage would be 0.65 per cent exactly with equal bets on each hand; but with a parabolic curve, the disadvantage is greater, at approximately 0.98 per cent. The reason for this is that the disadvantage from employing an increasingly inefficient basic strategy at low counts is not compensated by any additional advantage at high counts.

The second implication is that, if a player increases the bet in favourable situations *as if* the relationship between the true count and player advantage were linear, then he or she is likely to be overbetting. This implies that the player is vulnerable to the risk of ruin and may be one reason why skilful players of the game are wiped out, even when playing with an advantage over the dealer.

These two factors suggest that casinos have little to fear from players of basic strategy. Under UK rules, basic strategy players suffer an average disadvantage of 1 per cent with flat bets. Conversely, card counters who increase their bet on the basis of linear estimates of their advantage may, unwittingly, be overbetting their bankrolls, and leaving themselves open to ruin by a bad run of cards.

In either case, the casinos can confidently expect to win the bankrolls of basic strategy players over a long series of trials.

The Player's True Advantage Using the Optimal Playing Strategy

The limitations of basic strategy as a method of play suggest that the player must be more flexible in his or her play in order to succeed. Basic strategy is the strategy which maximizes the player's expectation against a standard deck, but it is inappropriate for a deck which is rich in either high or low cards. This fact, together with the practical constraints on large bet spreads, has led to greater emphasis in recent years on the analysis of variations in playing strategy to enhance the player's expectation.

As a general principle, the narrower the betting spread, the more important are variations in playing strategy. With bet spreads lower than 10, a player's expected return from the game can be significantly enhanced by judicious adjustments to the basic strategy of play.

Most of the literature of blackjack does not emphasize this point sufficiently. Basic strategy is usually compared favourably to two alternative strategies for play: 'mimic the dealer' and 'never draw to a stiff'.

'Mimic the dealer' involves the player doing whatever the dealer would do with a given hand. The player never doubles down or splits, and always draws to totals of 16 or less. The problem with the strategy is that, since the player draws first, he or she loses all hands which bust, even if the dealer busts subsequently. Since the player and dealer would both bust about 28 per cent of the time if they pursued this strategy, it would place the player at a disadvantage of approximately 8 per cent against the dealer ($=0.28 \times 0.28$). This disadvantage is reduced by the fact that the player is paid 3–2 on blackjacks. Despite this, the 'mimic the dealer' strategy remains distinctly unattractive under normal circumstances. According to Peter Griffin, the player's disadvantage adopting a 'mimic the dealer' strategy would be 5.5 percent.

The player labours under a similar disadvantage if he or she never draws to a stiff hand of between 12 and 16. This strategy, or something approximating it, is more common in actual casino play than imitating the dealer. However, the dealer busts only 28 per cent of the time, and if the dealer's first card is a 10 or an ace, then the chance of a dealer bust is less than 22 per cent. Consequently, if the dealer shows a high card, the player is better advised to draw on totals of between 12 and 16 in an effort to turn a losing hand into a winning one.

In normal circumstances, therefore, either imitating the dealer or never drawing to a stiff compares unfavourably with basic strategy.

However, it is not difficult to imagine abnormal circumstances where either strategy could be superior to basic strategy.

First, consider the case where the shoe contains only small cards waiting to be dealt, such as 2s, 3s, 4s and 5s. In a four-deck shoe, it is possible that situations close to this may occur at the end of the shoe on very rare occasions. The application of basic strategy in such a situation would place the player at a disadvantage of 100 per cent. The dealer would never bust, while it would be impossible for the basic strategy player to get more than 17 (the maximum total that would be achieved by drawing a 5 on a hard total of 12 against a dealer's 2 or 3). Thus, the best possible result for which a basic strategy player could hope would be a tie. Worse still, when the player doubled down on hard 9 or 10, or split two 2s or two 3s, he or she would be throwing good money after bad, since these options would result in further losses. Playing basic strategy in such circumstances would be disastrous.

By contrast, the player who imitated the dealer by never doubling or splitting, and always drawing to hard 16 or less, would enjoy a fair game, with a 50 per cent chance of winning each hand, and an even money pay-off.

If the undealt shoe contained aces as well as small cards, then the player who imitated the dealer but drew to soft 17 (while the dealer, under British rules, has to stand) would actually enjoy an advantage over the house, even though the true count was very negative.

Conversely, when the true count is positive and very high, a strategy of never drawing to a hard total of between 12 and 16 may be superior to basic strategy. Even against a strong dealer card such as 9, 10 or ace, the player's expectation with a stiff hand of 14, 15 or 16 may be maximized by standing, in the hope that the dealer will draw a low card and then bust.

The general point emerging from this analysis is that *there is no unique optimal playing strategy for blackjack*. While basic strategy is the optimal strategy against a randomly shuffled standard deck, something close to 'mimic the dealer' would be the optimal strategy if the deck only contained low cards, and 'never draw a stiff' would be a superior strategy if the deck only contained high cards. Computer simulations tend to confirm this result, by indicating that the player should alter the basic playing strategy towards 'mimic the dealer' as the true count gets lower, and towards 'never draw to a stiff' as the true count gets higher.

If the player does make appropriate variations in playing strategy according to the true count, then the rate of loss is less at very low counts than would be increased by a linear relationship between the true count and player advantage. Indeed, there may be situations in which the true count is very low (negative and less than -25) where the player is actually playing at an advantage. There is evidence that some players intuitively recognize this. In *Blackbelt in Blackjack*, Arnold Snyder describes the technique of 'depth charging', whereby card counters increase their bet as the deck is depleted even when the count is negative, and rely exclusively on changes in playing strategy to gain an edge over the dealer (I personally would not recommend this except possibly in single-deck games).

Similarly, the player can increase his or her advantage at very high counts by adjusting the playing strategy to draw less, and split and double down more, than with basic strategy. However, the relationship is not symmetrical between high and low counts. At negative counts, the difference between the theoretically optimal strategy and basic strategy could reach 100 per cent. Conversely, at very high positive counts, the deck structure itself places limits on possible playing errors. A player could only be at a 100 per cent disadvantage to the dealer by taking decisions like drawing to a blackjack or to totals of between 18 and 21, which no basic strategist would ever do. The deck structure also places upper limits on the maximum advantage that a player could secure over the dealer.

The central conclusions of this analysis are as follows:

1   The relationship in casino blackjack between the player's advantage and the true count is non-linear.
2   The reason for this non-linearity is that the optimal playing strategy is not constant, but is continuously changing as the deck is depleted. In particular, although basic strategy is the most efficient playing strategy against a randomly shuffled standard deck of cards, it becomes increasingly inefficient as the true count diverges from zero.
3   As a corollary of point 2, the average disadvantage for the basic strategy player who is betting a fixed sum on each hand is not equal to the estimated disadvantage off the top of the deck, but is somewhat higher. In the case of a player playing basic strategy under British casino rules, the average disadvantage is not 0.65 per cent, but approximately 0.98 per cent.
4   A player who bets as though the relationship between the true count and the player advantage is linear may unintentionally be overbetting the true advantage that he or she enjoys. This tendency to overbet may be one reason why skilful players are vulnerable to the risk of ruin.

5 Conversely, with appropriate modifications in playing strategy, the player's disadvantage at very low (negative) counts may not be as great as implied by a simple linear relationship, and in certain circumstances the player may actually be able to gain an edge over the dealer under these conditions. Modifications in playing strategy can also enhance the player's advantage at positive true counts.

6 Consequently, players who are able to adjust the playing strategy to take into account changes in the structure of the undealt cards can significantly reduce the disadvantage under which they play. In the case of a player applying optimal strategy under British casino rules, I calculate that the average disadvantage is reduced from about 0.98 per cent applying basic strategy to about 0.33 per cent, placing flat bets. The exact reduction will depend on the depth of the cut card, which will determine how often a card-counting player is likely to vary the playing strategy.

Appendix III

Mathematical Expectation in Baccarat

Bets and Pay-offs in Baccarat

In casino baccarat (punto banco), the gambler's only choices are how much to bet, and whether the bet should be placed on the punto (player) or banco (banker) hands. Winning punto bets are paid off at even money, while winning banco bets are paid off at slightly less than even money, or 0.95–1.

These differential pay-offs sometimes lead the uniniated gambler to suppose that a punto bet is superior to a banco bet. In fact, this is not the case; the banco bet has a greater expectation of winning. Banco's edge more than offsets the 5 per cent commission taken by the casino on winning banco hands. The gambler's expectation on both punto and banco hands is negative, but it is less negative on the banco than the punto hand. The percentage expectations are as follows:

Bet	Pay-off	Bettor's edge (%)	% of plays
Punto (player)	1–1	−1.23	44.62
Banco (bank)	0.95–1	−1.06	45.86
Tie	9–1	−14.36	9.52

Sources: Edward O. Thorp, *The Mathematics of Gambling*; Peter Griffin, *The Theory of Blackjack*

The tie bet is not normally offered in British casinos. Even if it were, the gambler would be ill advised to take it, since it has a negative expectation of more than 14 per cent.

If the hands are tied (which occurs on slightly less than one out of every ten hands) then any bets on punto and banco stand, and no money changes hands. In this respect, ties in baccarat are treated identically to ties in blackjack.

The Rules of Baccarat

After all bets have been placed, the croupier will instruct whoever is acting as banco to deal the cards face-up in the following sequence:

1st card to the player (punto)
2nd card to the banker (banco)
3rd card to the player (punto)
4th card to the banker (banco)

After the first four cards have been dealt, the rules of the game are mechanical, with neither side enjoying any discretion in how the hands are played. This represents the most significant difference between baccarat and blackjack, since the great attraction of blackjack is precisely that it is the one casino game in which the player can exercise skill.

If punto's first two cards total 8 (i.e. 8 or 18) or 9 (9 or 19), then punto has a natural winner and wins outright (unless banco ties by also drawing a two-card total of 8 or 9). Conversely, if banco has a two-card total of 8 or 9, then banco wins outright with no further cards drawn.

In the event that neither punto nor banco draws a natural, play proceeds with punto having the first opportunity to draw a third card. If punto's first two cards total 6 or 7, then punto stands. These totals are strong, but do not win outright. If punto has any other total, i.e. any total between 0 and 5, then punto must draw in an attempt to improve the hand.

In summary, the rules for punto's play are as follows:

If punto has . . .	Then punto . . .
1, 2, 3, 4, 5, 10 (0)	Draws a card
6, 7	Stands
8, 9	Stands – and banco cannot draw either

Once punto's play is complete, banco has a chance to respond.

If punto has a natural two-card 8 or 9 and banco does not, then punto wins outright. If punto has a two-card 6 or 7, then banco draws on any two-card total between 0 and 5, but stands on 6 or 7.

If punto has drawn a third card, banco's response is as follows. Banco must draw if its two-card total is 0, 1 or 2. Banco also draws with a two-card total of 3, unless punto's third card was an 8, in which case banco stands.

Banco's other rules for drawing are somewhat more complex. With a total of 4, banco draws if punto's third card was between 2 and 7, and stands if punto's third card was 8, 9 or 10 (including picture cards with a value of 0) or an ace (with a value of 1).

With a total of 5, banco draws if punto's third card was between 4 and 7, but stands if punto's third card was less than 4 or 8 or 9.

With a total of 6, banco draws if punto's third card was 6 or 7, but stands in all other cases.

Banco always stands with a two-card total of 7; and either ties or wins outright with a two-card natural of 8 or 9.

In summary, the rules for banco if punto has drawn a third card are as follows:

If banco has . . .	After punto draws a third card of . . .	Then banco . . .
0, 1 or 2	Anything	Draws
3	Anything other than 8	Draws
4	2, 3, 4, 5, 6 or 7	Draws
4	0, 1, 8 or 9	Stands
5	4, 5, 6 or 7	Draws
5	0–3, 8 or 9	Stands
6	6 or 7	Draws
6	0–5, 8 or 9	Stands
7	Anything	Stands

These rules are played automatically under the supervision of the casino umpire. In fact, anyone who plays baccarat for any length of time will pick up the rules as they go, although it is not necessary to do so.

The Influence of Different Cards in Baccarat

The rules for playing baccarat appear complicated, but a little reflection indicates that they are tilted slightly in banco's favour. This can be seen particularly with banco's rules for drawing with two-card totals of 3, 4, 5 or 6. The playing rules dictate that banco is more likely to stand on winning totals than on losing totals; while banco's rules for drawing also slightly improve its chances of winning.

For example, banco only stands on 3 if punto has drawn an 8 as its third card. Punto in turn will only have drawn on a two-card total of between 0 and 5, so an 8 will leave punto with a total of 8 or 9 (if drawn on a two-card total of 0 or 1), or between 0 and 3 (if drawn on a two-card total of between 2 and 5). Of these six possibilities, banco loses to punto's three-card 8 or 9; wins against punto's three-card 0, 1 or 2; and ties against punto's three-card 3. Banco's rule of standing on 3 if punto has just drawn an 8 thus gives banco a 60–40 edge (ignoring ties).

With a total of 4, banco stands if punto's third card is an 8, 9, 10 or ace, and draws otherwise. Since punto only draws on two-card totals of between 0 and 5, the chances are that if punto's third card was 8, 9, 10 or ace, then banco's two-card 4 will win or tie. Similar considerations apply to banco's rules for drawing on a two-card total of 5 or 6. In all cases, the rules imply that banco is more likely to stand if its two-card total is winning, and to draw if its two-card is losing.

Further reflection indicates that, in the final draw after the first two cards have been dealt to each side, certain cards will favour punto, while others will favour banco. Punto draws a third card if its two-card total is between 0 and 5; to improve this hand, punto would generally wish to draw a small card such as 2, 3 or 4. High cards will not generally help: a 10 would leave the value of the hand unaffected, while a 9 diminishes all two-card punto hands except 0, and an 8 diminishes all two-card punto hands except 0 or 1. The best card for punto is a 4, since this will improve all the two-card totals on which punto draws, and will transform two-card totals of 4 or 5 into three-card totals of 8 or 9 which will usually win.

Conversely, banco benefits if high cards are drawn by punto. If punto draws a high third card, it will in general diminish punto's hand rather than improve it. Banco does not draw on 4, 5 or 6 if punto's third card is an 8, 9 or 10, and in these cases usually stands with a two-card winning total. Equally, on the occasions when banco must draw a third card – that is, when banco's two-card total is 0, 1 or 2 – banco is most helped by a high card. The most helpful card for banco is in fact a 6, since this improves all banco's low hands.

These considerations led me to consider whether it might be possible to develop a winning card-counting system for casino baccarat or punto banco.

From Professor Griffin's *Theory of Blackjack*, I derived an 'ultimate point count' which I developed into a usable card count as follows:

| | My point count[1] | Griffin's Ultimate Point Count | |
		Punto	Banco
ace	1	−1.86	+1.82
2	1	−2.25	+2.28
3	1a	−2.79	+2.69
4	2a	−4.96	+4.80
5	−1a	+3.49	−3.43
6	−2a	+4.69	−4.70
7	−1a	+3.39	−3.44
8	−1	+2.21	−2.08
9	0	+1.04	−0.96
10	0	+0.74	+0.78
jack	0	−0.74	+0.78
queen	0	−0.74	+0.78
king	a	−0.74	+0.78

[1] In my point count, 'a' indicates a value of 0.5

My point count is approximately 50 per cent of Griffin's Ultimate Point Count.

I devised the following betting schedule:

| Positive counts | | Negative counts | |
True count	Bet	True count	Bet
+15<TC<25	1 unit on banco	−15>TC>−25	1 unit on punto
+25<TC<35	2 units on banco	−25>TC>−35	2 units on punto
+35<TC	3 units on banco	−35>TC	3 units on punto

The application of the system is described in 'Can Baccarat be Beaten?' (pp. 125–7). Although it won modest amounts of money over a small series of trials, I consider it very difficult to apply under actual casino conditions. My overall conclusion was that, while the attempt to beat baccarat was not without intellectual interest, there are much easier ways of making money, even in a casino.

Glossary

Action The total amount of money bet by gamblers in a casino game. For example, if a gambler placed 150 bets of £5 each his or her total action would be £750.

Ante A bet placed before the first card is dealt in a game such as poker or blackjack.

'Anted away' The process whereby a poker player can lose his entire bankroll by placing ante bets and then throwing in poor hands.

Back counting The process by which a card-counting blackjack player counts down a deck or shoe of cards without playing at the table (usually by standing at the back of the players at the table), with the intention of betting only when the deck becomes favourable. Also known as Wonging, after Stanford Wong, the gambler who first popularized the technique.

Bankroll The total playing stake of a player or team.

Basic strategy The mathematically optimal way for a blackjack player to play his or her hands against a randomly shuffled deck or shoe of cards, defined as that method of play which, given the rules of the game, maximizes the expected gain or minimizes the expected loss in any situation. See Appendix II.

Bernoulli system A closed mathematical system, such as roulette or dice games, where each result has a constant probability from one trial to another, the results of each trial are mutually exclusive and independent of each other, and the sum of the probabilities of all possible outcomes is 100 per cent.

Bernoulli theorem The rule that the larger the number of trials within a Bernoulli system, the more likely it is that the actual results will approximate their mathematical expectation. Also known as the law of large numbers.

Betting box See **Box**.

Bet spread   The ratio of the bets placed by a blackjack player in favourable situations compared to unfavourable situations. Thus, if a blackjack player places a bet of 5 units when the cards are in his favour, and 1 unit otherwise, his or her bet spread is 5–1.

Betting system   A series of mathematical rules determining how a gambler should allocate his capital between wagers on different trials in a game.

Blackjack (or natural)   A blackjack is the best possible hand in blackjack, comprising an ace (valued at 11) and a 10 or court card (valued at 10), to give a two-card total of 21. This hand is a natural winner, and for this reason is also known as a natural. Only the first two cards dealt may form a blackjack; it cannot be formed from values of 21 resulting from split aces.

Box   A square area on the blackjack table in front of the player in which he or she places a bet. Typically, a UK blackjack table has between seven and ten boxes, and more than one person is permitted to place a bet in each box (although responsibility for the playing decision remains with the first person to bet in the box).

Bust   A worthless card hand, on which any money bet is lost.

Busting   The process of drawing a card that destroys the hand being played, and makes it a certain loser: e.g., in blackjack, drawing a card that takes the value of the hand above 21.

Card counting   The process of keeping track of the cards as they are dealt out in blackjack or baccarat, to assess the composition of the cards remaining to be dealt and calculate the probability of a player or dealer win.

Central limit theorem   The statistical rule that, as the sample size is increased, so the sampling distribution approaches the normal distribution in form.

Conversion factor   The number by which the running count in blackjack is divided to arrive at the true or exact count. It is equal to the number of full decks or half decks that have not yet been played.

Count (or running count)   The cumulative value of all cards played at any given time, based on a set of preassigned values for each card denomination (see **Point count**).

Counter   A blackjack player who uses a counting system to keep track of the cards played in order to determine whether the deck is favourable or unfavourable.

Court cards   The jack, queen or king, all of which have a value of 10 in blackjack and 0 in baccarat.

Croupier A casino employee who spins the roulette wheel and collects or settles up bets placed on the roulette table.

Cut card A card, usually a solid coloured piece of plastic, inserted into the cards in a deck or shoe to determine at what point they will be shuffled.

Dealer A casino employee operating on the blackjack or baccarat tables who deals the cards, makes the pay-offs, sees the rules are followed at the table, and plays his own hand on behalf of the casino according to a fixed set of rules.

De Moivre's theorem The rule that, during a series of trials within a Bernoulli system, the actual results will fluctuate from the mathematically expected result in proportion to the square root of the number of trials.

Dealer's bias A bias in the ordering of a deck or shoe of cards favouring the dealer.

Doubling (or double down) An option that allows a blackjack player to double the value of his or her bet after looking at the first two cards. In the UK, the player is only allowed to double if the first two cards have a combined value of 9, 10 or 11, and is then only allowed to receive one additional card.

Double the bank The objective of many card counters or teams: to double their original playing stake or bankroll and then quit.

Draw To request additional cards from the dealer to add to the original cards dealt.

Drop The total amount of cash, cheques and markers taken by a casino from all gamblers for a game or shift.

Exact count (or true count) The exact count is equal to the running count divided by the conversion factor. It indicates what the count would be if the game were being dealt from a single deck. Thus, if the running count is 12, and three decks remain to be dealt, the exact count is $(12/3) = 4$, indicating to the player that there is a relative surplus of two 10s (or a deficit of two 4s, 5s or 6s) per 52 cards left to be dealt. The player can then adjust his bet and playing strategy to reflect this information.

Expected value The money that the player should win (or lose) given average luck: that is, in exact accordance with statistical advantage. Expected value = player's advantage (in per cent) multiplied by total action.

Face card (or court card) A king, queen or jack. All face cards have the same value of 10 in blackjack.

Fair game A game in which the pay-offs are equal to the mathematical chances of winning. Casino games are not fair if the gambler plays randomly, since the casino's pay-offs are slightly less than the mathematical probability of each result, and this small advantage will prove decisive over a long series of trials.

First base   A term to describe the far right-hand seat at the blackjack table. The first base is the first player to be dealt a card.

Flat bet   To bet the same amount of money on each hand played. Over a long period, it is impossible to beat the game of blackjack (at least as offered under UK rules) by placing flat bets and relying on variations in playing strategy alone, because the dealer is bound to win most hands since he or she draws last and the player loses a bust hand, even if the dealer also busts.

Folding   Throwing in a hand of cards, e.g. in poker.

Gambler's fallacy   The erroneous belief that because an event has not occurred recently in a series of independent trials, it becomes more likely to occur in the future.

Gambler's ruin   The risk that a gambler will tap out, or lose his entire bankroll, even when playing in a positive expectation game, if he overbets a limited bankroll and suffers a negative fluctuation.

Gaming Board   The government-appointed authority regulating casino gambling in Britain.

Hard hand   Blackjack hands that do not include an ace, or in which ace can only be valued as 1 if the total value of the hand is not to exceed 21.

Head-on (or head-to-head)   A game in which the player plays alone against the dealer. In British casinos, a player playing head-to-head against the dealer must play at least two hands in each round.

Heat   Actions or statements by casino personnel that lead the player to believe he is suspected of being a counter and may be barred from the casino.

Hit   To request another card from the dealer.

Hold   The ratio between the amount won by the casino, and the drop or total amount of cash and cheques changed into chips by the gamblers.

Hole card   A card dealt face-down or concealed in blackjack or poker. In Britain, it refers to the dealer's second card, always dealt after all the players have completed their hands.

Insurance   A bet in blackjack equal to half the original bet that can be placed by a player who is dealt a blackjack if the dealer's first card is an ace. The bet 'insures' against the possibility that the dealer gets a blackjack by offering a 2–1 pay-off if he does so.

Joint bankroll An arrangement in blackjack and other games whereby two or more gamblers combine resources and play jointly off the total amount, sharing any wins or losses. The advantage of the arrangement is that it reduces fluctuations in the bankroll, and provides the psychological support a lone gambler lacks.

Maximum boldness strategy The strategy of gambling aggressively for a limited period which gives the gambler the best chance of success in a negative-expectation game such as single-zero roulette.

Minimax principle The strategy of selecting the option minimizing the maximum risk in any situation.

Minus count A cumulative negative count of the cards dealt in the game of blackjack, which indicates that a surplus of high cards has been dealt, so that the remainder of the shoe contains a surplus of low cards (to the disadvantage of the player).

Money management The art of managing one's bankroll to derive the maximum possible advantage from it.

Mug punter A gambler who lacks even a rudimentary knowledge of the odds and probabilities in a game in which he participates.

Multiple deck A blackjack game played with more than one deck of cards: usually between two and six decks. In the UK, all games are dealt from four-deck shoes.

Natural An automatic two-card winner, comprising an ace-10 (10 or court card) which totals 21 in blackjack, or a two-card total or 8 of 9 in baccarat.

Negative swing A period during which a player shows a loss, even when playing with a mathematical advantage, because of statistical deviation from the expected (mean) result.

Normal distribution A distribution of actual results around the expected or average outcome which is symmetrical and bell-shaped, with an equal number of positive and negative deviations from the average result.

Octant A group of any five numbers which are physically adjacent around a roulette wheel.

Off-the-top At the beginning of a shoe of cards, immediately after the shuffle.

Pair splitting See Splitting.

Pat hand A hand in blackjack totalling between 17 and 21. A player can expect to be dealt a pat hand with the first two cards totalling between 17 and 21 approximately a third (33 per cent) of the time. In such cases, the player will almost always stand (stand pat).

Pit boss   A casino official who supervises play at a group of gaming tables.

Player's advantage   The per cent of money bet that a player can expect to win in the long run. If a player enjoys a 1 per cent advantage, he will in the long run win 1 per cent of the total amount of money bet. If the player's expectation is −5 per cent, he will eventually lose £5 of every £100 bet. Most blackjack players play with a disadvantage of between −5 per cent and −1 per cent under UK rules, depending on their level of skill. Even the most skilful card counter is unlikely to secure an advantage of more than +1 per cent for any length of time, unless he or she uses a very high bet spread, which could arouse suspicion and lead to being barred from a casino.

Player's bias   A bias in the ordering of deck or shoe of cards favouring the player.

Point count   The evaluation of odds in blackjack via a tally of assigned points. A number is assigned to each card indicating the extent to which the removal of the card helps or hinders the player. In general, the removal of small cards helps the players and the removal of high cards (10s count cards and aces) helps the dealer. Thus, point count systems assign positive values to low cards, and negative values to high cards. In the main or zen count, 2s, 3s and 7s are assigned a count value of +1; 4s, 5s and 6s are assigned a value of +2; 10s (including court cards) have a value of −2; and aces a value of −1; with 8s and 9s not counted (i.e. having a value of 0). The point count is computed by adding the counts for each card played in that hand to the point count at the end of the previous hand. Thus, at all times the card counter has a single running count in his head.

Poor   The shoe is said to be poor in certain values of cards if there is a smaller than normal percentage of that card value present.

Population standard deviation   The standard deviation of a sample of trials.

Press   To increase the size of a subsequent wager, normally by letting a winning bet remain in the betting box.

Probability   The probability of an event is the extent to which it is likely to occur, measured by the ratio of favourable cases to all possible cases. Mathematically, the probability of an event $x = x/n$, where x = the actual occurrences of the event, and n = all possible occurrences in the observed sample. Thus, if x occurs 50,000 times in a sample of 1,000,000, its probability is 0.05 or 5 per cent.

Push See **Tie**.

Rich The shoe is said to be rich in certain values of cards if there is a larger than normal percentage of that card value present.

Risk of ruin The percentage likelihood that the gambler will tap out (or lose his entire bankroll) within a defined period or before achieving a specified goal such as doubling the bankroll.

Running count The cumulative value of all cards played at any given time based on a set of preassigned values for each card denomination (see **Point count**).

Shoe The dealing box from which the cards are dealt on blackjack tables, placed on the dealer's left and the player's right. In UK and Monte Carlo casinos, all shoes contain four decks of cards at the beginning of play; on the French Riviera and in Holland and Belgium, blackjack is dealt from a six-deck shoe.

Shuffle tracking The process by which a card player seeks to follow certain cards as they are shuffled, in order to identify when they are likely to appear in the reshuffled deck or shoe of cards.

Soft hand A hand which includes an ace and has a total value of 11 or less if the ace is valued as 1. A player cannot bust by drawing to a soft hand.

Splitting A player can split if he receives two cards of equal value as his first two cards by separating them and playing them as separate hands. In order to indicate that he or she wishes to split, the player has to place a bet equal to the original wager alongside it in the betting box. Under British rules, a player is not allowed to split 4s, 5s, or 10s, and if he splits aces is only allowed to draw one more card on each ace. For other cards, he may draw as many extra cards as he wishes, and double down a split hand which has a hard value of 9, 10 or 11 after a second card is placed on it.

Stacking Setting up the cards in a deck in a pre-arranged order in order to manipulate the results of a game. An example is the high-low stack where high cards are sequentially interleaved with low cards, allowing the dealer to select either a high or low card according to whether he draws the top card or second card.

Stand A player's decision not to draw additional cards.

Stand-off. See **Tie**.

Standard deviation The mathematically normal fluctuation from an expected result.

Steaming   A losing gambler placing ever larger bets in an effort to recoup his losses.

Stiff hand   A hand in blackjack totalling between 12 and 16. A player can expect to be dealt a stiff hand with the first two cards totalling between 12 and 16 approximately 37 per cent of the time. In such cases, the player should sometimes stand and sometimes draw, depending on what card the dealer shows and what composition of remaining cards is indicated by the true count.

Strike number   The true count in a counting system at which the size of the bet or the play of the hand is varied. For example, using the main count the strike number for standing on 12 against a dealer's 2 is +5: if the exact count is less than +5, the player should draw; if it is greater (indicating a surplus of high cards), he should stand.

Surrender   Surrender is an option allowed in certain American casinos, though not in British casinos: a player can return his first two cards for a forfeit of half his initial bet before the dealer plays, provided that the dealer does not have a blackjack.

Table hopping   When a card-counting blackjack player moves from table to table and places bets only when he observes that a number of small cards have been dealt out, leading him to conclude that there is a higher than average proportion of high cards waiting to be dealt.

Tap out   To lose one's entire bank.

Third base   A term to describe the far left-hand seat at the blackjack table, who is the last person to play before the dealer.

Tie   A hand in which both the player and dealer hold cards with the same total value when their hands are completed. In the event of a tie, no money changes hands. It is also known as a push or stand-off.

True count   A ratio used by card-counting blackjack players indicating the proportion of high cards to low cards waiting to be dealt from a deck or shoe. See **Exact count**.

Value-for-money bet   A bet where the true probability of a result is greater than the odds being offered against the result. In blackjack, all bets are even-money bets, so if the player has a better than even chance of beating the dealer for any hand, he or she is being offered a value-for-money bet.

References

The Development of the Casino Industry

Barnhart, Russell T., 'Gambling in Revolutionary Paris: The Palais Royal 1789–1838', paper presented to the Ninth International Conference on Risk and Gambling, Kensington, London, August 1990
– *Gamblers of Yesteryear*, GBC Press, Las Vegas, 1983
Corti, Count Egon, *Der Zauberer von Homburg und Monte Carlo*, Leipzig, 1932
'Goodbye Mr Chips', *Investors' Chronicle*, 14 June 1991
'Mayfair's Weak Hand', *Economist*, 16 June 1991
'Aspinall's bid for new casino licence comes up trumps', *London Evening Standard*, 28 June 1991
Tomkinson, Martin, 'Gentlemen and Players', *Business*, August 1989
Wolfe, Tom, 'Las Vegas', *The Kandy-Kolored Tangerine-Flake Streamline Baby*, Jonathan Cape, London, 1966

Roulette

Barnhart, Russell T., *Gamblers of Yesteryear*, GBC Press, Las Vegas, Nevada, 1983
Bass, Thomas, *The Newtonian Casino*, Longman, London, 1990
Beresford, the Hon. S. R., *Beresford's Monte Carlo*, Nice, 1926
Corti, Count Egon, *Der Zauberer von Homburg und Monte Carlo*, Leipzig, 1932
Dostoevsky, Fyodor, *The Gambler*, Penguin Books, London, 1966
Payne, Stewart and Nigel Rosser, 'Lady's Luck was a £750,000 Sting', *London Evening Standard*, 20 June 1991
Rosslyn, James Francis Harry, 5th Earl of, *My Gamble with Life*, New York, 1928
Sala, George Augustus, *The Life and Adventures of George Augustus Sala* (2 vols), New York, 1895
Sirven, Alfred, *Les Tripots d'Allemagne*, Paris, 1863

Soares, John, *Loaded Dice: The True Story of a Casino Cheat*, Star Books, London, 1988

Thorp, Dr Edward, 'Roulette', *The Mathematics of Gambling*, Gambling Times, 1984

Williamson, C. N., 'Systems and System Players at Monte Carlo', *McClure's Magazine*, Vol. 40, 1913

Blackjack

Andersen, Ian, *Turning the Tables on Las Vegas*, Vintage Books, New York, 1976

Baldwin, Roger, with Wilbert Cantey, Herbert Maisel and James MacDermott, 'The Optimum Strategy in Blackjack', *Journal of the American Statistical Association*, Vol. 51, 1956

Barnett, Ned, 'King of the Counters Holds Victory Court', *Atlantic City Press*, 12 May 1981

Braun, Julian, *The Development and Analysis of Winning Strategies for Casino Blackjack*, Chicago, Illinois, 1975

Braun, Julian, *How to Play Winning Blackjack*, Data House Publishing Co. Inc., Chicago, Illinois, 1980

Chambliss, C. R. and T. C. Roginski, *Playing Blackjack in Atlantic City*, GBC Press, Las Vegas, Nevada, 1981

– *The Fundamentals of Blackjack*, GBC Press, Las Vegas, Nevada, 1990

Diamond, Michael, 'Court supports card counters', *Atlantic City Press*, 12 May 1981

Epstein, Richard A., *The Theory of Gambling and Statistical Logic*, Academic Press, New York, 2nd edition, 1977

Goodman, Mike, *How to Win at Cards, Dice, Races and Roulette*, Holloway House Publishing Co., Los Angeles, 1963

– *Your Best Bet*, Brooke House, Northridge, California, 1975

Griffin, Peter, 'The Use of Bivariate Normal Approximations to Evaluate Single Parameter Card Counting Systems in Blackjack', paper presented to the Second Conference on Gambling, Lake Tahoe, June 1975

– *The Theory of Blackjack*, Huntington Press, Las Vegas, Nevada, 4th edition, 1988

– *Extra Stuff: Gambling Ramblings*, Huntington Press, Las Vegas, Nevada, 1991

Humble, Lance, *Blackjack Super Gold*, D & G Publishing Co. Inc., 1979

– and Carl Cooper, *The World's Greatest Blackjack Book*, Doubleday & Co., New York, revised edition, 1987

The International Casino Guide, B. D. I. T. Inc., Flushing, New York, 1989

Kelly, J. L., 'A New Interpretation of Information Rate', *Bell System Technical Journal*, Vol. 35, 1956

Patterson, Jerry L., *Blackjack: A Winner's Handbook*, Vorhees New Jersey, 1977, 1981

– *Blackjack's Winning Formula*, Perigee Books, New York, 1982
– and Eddie Olsen, *Break the Dealer*, Perigee Books, New York, 1986
Revere, Lawrence, *Playing Blackjack as a Business: A Textbook on Blackjack*, Lyle Stuart Inc., New Jersey, 1969, 1980
Snyder, Arnold, *The Blackjack Formula*, RGE Press, Berkeley, California, 1980
– *Blackjack for Profit*, RGE Press, Berkeley, California, 1981
– *Blackbelt in Blackjack*, RGE Press, Berkeley, California, 1983
– *Beat the Four-Deck Game*, RGE Press, Berkeley, California, 1987
Thorp, Edward O., 'Fortune's Formula: The Game of Blackjack', *Notices of the American Mathematical Society*, December, 1960
– 'A Favourable Strategy for Twenty-one', *Proceedings of the National Academy of Science*, Vol. 47, No. 1, 1961
– *Beat the Dealer*, Vintage Books, New York, 2nd edition, 1966
– 'The Principles of the Game and Why it Can be Beaten', in Stanley Roberts (ed.), *Gambling Times Guide to Blackjack*, Lyle Stuart Inc., New Jersey, 1984
– 'Blackjack', Chapter 2 in *The Mathematics of Gambling*, Gambling Times, California, 1984
Tulcea, C. Ionescu, *A Book on Casino Blackjack*, Van Nostrand Reinhold Company Inc., 1982
Uston, Ken, *One Third of a Shoe*, Uston Institute of Blackjack, 1979
– *Ken Uston's Newsletters on Blackjack 1979–1981*, Uston Institute of Blackjack, 1981
– *Million Dollar Blackjack*, Gambling Times, California, 1981
– 'Does the Gaming Industry Have (or Need) a Conscience?' paper presented to the Fifth International Conference on Risk and Gambling, 1981
– Interview with Snyder, *Blackjack Forum*, June 1983
– 'Team Play and other advanced techniques', in Stanley Roberts (ed.), *Gambling Times Guide to Blackjack*, Lyle Stuart Inc., New Jersey, 1984
von Neumann and Oscar Morgenstern, *Theory of Games and Economic Behavior*, Princeton University Press, 1944
Wong, Stanford, *Professional Blackjack*, Pi Yee Press, California, 1975, 1981

Other Games

Baccarat

Griffin, Peter, 'Can Baccarat be Beaten?', pp. 216–19 in *The Theory of Blackjack*, Huntington Press, Las Vegas, Nevada, 4th edition, 1988
Jones, J. Philip, *Gambling Yesterday and Today*, David & Charles, London, 1973
Nolan, Walter I., *The Facts of Baccarat*, Gamblers Book Club, Las Vegas, Nevada, 1976
Sklansky, David, 'Card Counting and Baccarat', pp. 166–70 in *Getting the Best of It*, California, 1989

Spanier, David, *Easy Money: Inside the Gambler's Mind*, Secker & Warburg, London, 1987
Thorp, Dr Edward, 'Baccarat', *The Mathematics of Gambling*, Gambling Times, 1984

Poker
Alvarez, Al, *The Biggest Game in Town*, Andre Deutsch, London, 1983
Holden, Anthony, *Big Deal: One Year as a Professional Poker Player*, Bantam Press, London and New York, 1990
Yardley, Herbert O., *The Education of a Poker Player*, Oldcastle Books, Herts, 1957, 1990

Epilogue

Bradshaw, Jon, *Fast Company*, Vintage Books, New York, 1987
Davis, Jonathan, 'Three Rules for Getting Rich', *Financial Times*, 22/23 June 1991
Parris, Matthew, 'A Leader of Enduring Qualities', *Investors' Chronicle*, London, 5 July 1991
Train, John, *The Midas Touch*, Harper & Row, New York, 1987

Appendices

Epstein, Richard, *The Theory of Gambling and Statistical Logic*, Academic Press, New York, 1976
Griffin, Peter, 'On the Likely Consequences of Errors in Card Counting Systems', Mathematics Department, Sacramento State University, Sacramento, California, 1976
Kelly, J. L., 'A New Interpretation of Information Rate', *Bell System Technical Journal*, 1956
Snyder, Arnold, 'The "Best" Counting System', *Blackjack Forum*, September 1982
– and John Gwynn, 'How True is Your True Count?' *Blackjack Forum*, September 1982

Indexes

Names, places, subjects

The Knights of the Green Baize Tables

The Scenes of their Jousts

The Weapons They Used